Checkpoint Charlie

Ost-Berliner flüchtete in amerikanischer Uniform

Vopos verwickelten ihn 15 Minuten lang in ein Gespräch — aber er sprach besser Englisch als sie

(Fortsetzung vo...)

Im Wirtshaus Mo...
richtete Kellner Re...
weiter, habe er dem...
nen blauen Monte...
und Pullover ausge...
binden abgenomm...
als Kälteschutz zu...
Pulsadern gewick...
unter die lauwar...
stellt. "Liefern d...
be Jürgen K. stä...
immer voller A...
konnte ihn ber...
sei man sicher...
te die Feuerwe...
mit Unterkühl...
fer Behring-K...

Die "DDR"...
die Flucht of...
einer Stunde...
war ein Wac...
neben der...
setzt. Erst...
zwei Patrouillenboo...
Armee ein.

Berlin, 4. 11. 82

Dramatische Flucht am Ausländer-Übergang Checkpoint Charlie in der Friedrichstraße in Kreuzberg: In einer amerikanischen Uniform gelang es einem "DDR"-Bürger, einen Grenzwächter zu überlisten.

Es war am 23. Oktober um 14 Uhr 30. Ein US-Soldat kam aus Ost-Berlin und wollte die Grenze passieren. Wie bei den Alliierten üblich, rechnete er damit, nicht kontrolliert zu werden.

Aber diesmal waren die Vopos mißtrauisch. Sie hiel-

ten den Mann in der Uniform' an, weil er zu Fuß kam. Er mußte mit in die Baracke und zahlreiche Fragen über sich ergehen lassen.

Doch der Flüchtling...
d...
du...
sch...
gel...
De...
W...
Flü...
zei...
kep...

gen. Er meldete sich bei der Wache.

Als die Beamten den "Amerikaner" fragten, woher er... komme, antwort...

...kpoint Charlie

...ber die...
...harf be...
...e jeder...
...hörte zu...
...die die...
...punktes...
...ungsver...

...m Lauf...
...latz ist...
...st-Berlin...
...e zu er...
...tzten 20...
...chtling...
...reichen...
...pte, Brat...
...von der...
...bei, de...
...Grenz...
...erfolger...

...Check...
...zeugen...

der Flucht. Die westlichen Zöllner nahmen Bratke, der am ganzen Körper zitterte und unter Schockwirkung stand, in Empfang. Sie veranlaßten, daß er in ein Krankenhaus überführt wurde. Dort bekam Bratke eine Beruhigungsspritze.

"Die letzten 20 Meter von der Mauer bis zum Zoll hatte ich Todesangst", berichtete der Flüchtling der Zeitung BZ. Schon einige Tage vor dem gelungenen Versuch habe er die Absicht zur Flucht gehabt — "damals traute ich mich jedoch nicht". Bratke, dessen Eltern und Geschwister im Ostberliner Neubaubezirk Marzahn wohnen, hofft, daß er bald wieder Arbeit als Fernmeldemonteur findet.

Am streng gesicherten Checkpoint Charlie hat es seit dem Mauerbau 1961 relativ wenige Fluchtversuche gegeben. Ähnlich wie jetzt Bratke — im Laufschritt — war 1961, drei Monate nach dem Mauerbau, dem Bildreporter einer Ostberliner Zeitung am Checkpoint die Flucht gelungen.

Ein Mann bricht durch die Mauer

ASD Berlin

Der 21jährige Hans-Dieter Vollbrecht, dem in der Nacht zum Donnerstag im Kugelhagel der Zonengrenzposten die Flucht zum Potsdam-Babelsberg in den Westberliner Ortsteil Steinstücken geglückt ist, schildert die dramatischen Umstände und die Motive seiner Flucht:

"Ich habe es schon einmal versucht. Ende Mai 1974 über Ungarn. Damals wurde ich mit einem Kameraden drei Kilometer vor der jugoslawischen Grenze festgenommen und zu drei Jahren Zuchthaus verurteilt."

Seine dreijährige Zuchthausstrafe hat er bis auf den letzten Tag in der Jugendstrafanstalt in Torgau verbüßen müssen. Danach sei er unter Polizeiaufsicht gestellt worden, ein "Volkspolizist" hatte einen zweiten Schlüssel zu seiner Wohnung und konnte ihn zu jeder Tages- und Nachtzeit kontrollieren. "Einmal kam er morgens um zwei Uhr, als ich mit einer Freundin im Bett lag", erinnert sich Vollbrecht.

Außerdem wurde ihm ein Arbeitsplatz zugewiesen, den er zwei Jahre nicht wechseln durfte. In seinem Beruf als Getriebeschlosser arbeitete er bis zu seiner Flucht im Babelsberger "Karl-Marx-Werk" für 590 Mark netto im Monat.

"Alles das hat mich regelmä...

Hans-Dieter Vollbrecht nach der Flucht im Rollstuhl

Schlauch von Stacheldrahtzäunen nach West-Berlin fahren", berichtet Vollbrecht. "Als sich ein Güterzug näherte, kletterte ich über den Zaun. Die drei Lagen Stacheldraht bog ich zur Seite und sprang auf die andere Seite.

Dort fiel ich direkt auf die 'Fakirmatte'. Das sind über ein Meter breite Bretter mit mindestens zehn Zentimeter langen Dornen. Mit dem linken Fuß trat ich direkt in einen der spitzen Eisenstachel."

"Nun rannte ich dem Güterzug hinterher. Etwa hundert Meter bevor der Zaun auf die Mauer stößt und Schienen nach Steinstücken hineinreichen, rief eine Stimme plötzlich: 'Halt, stehenbleiben!'. Ich lief um mein Leben: Das war ein neuer 100-Meter-Rekord."

"Ich hörte die Kugeln der Vopos in die Mauer neben mir schlagen. Es war ein Feuerstoß mit sieben oder zehn Schüssen. Dann war ich in Steinstücken. Ich lief noch ein paar hundert Meter und ließ mich dann fallen, um zu verschnaufen. Als ich in Steinstücken war und es geschafft hatte, habe ich geheult wie ein kleiner Junge. Ich bin erst mal zusammengebrochen."

Er sagt: "Ich bin froh, nun end...

ESCAPE FROM BERLIN

ESCAPE
FROM
BERLIN

ANTHONY KEMP

First published in 1987 by Boxtree Limited

Text copyright © Anthony Kemp 1987

ISBN 1 85283 202 9

Printed and bound in Great Britain by
Butler & Tanner Ltd, Frome and London
for Boxtree Limited
25 Floral Street
London WC2E 9DS

Contents

Acknowledgements

The writing of a book of this type presupposes the help of many people. During the many weeks I spent in Berlin and in West Germany I was granted help on a massive scale and much kindness and hospitality. I list below those private persons and organisations without whom neither the original film nor the resulting book could have been produced. They are not placed in any order of merit and I offer my humble apologies for anyone I may have omitted.

My employer, Television South and Peter Williams, Head of Factual Programmes, made it possible for me to undertake the lengthy task of research, and all of us were given a useful shove in the right direction by Alan Shadrake. Much of the time I was accompanied by Gordon Stevens, friend and film director, who once again had to put up with constant history lectures. We were both lucky in having an excellent crew with us who not only made a fine film but considerably enriched the proprietor of the 'Irish Bar' in the Europa Centre. Wolfgang Fuchs and his family not only helped on the factual side but provided unstinting hospitality and friendship. Wolf Quasner taught me about the finer points of forgery and Helmut Sonntag and his colleague, Ernst Wollenberg, allowed us to view their extensive collection of archive film. Anybody researching into the history of the Berlin wall owes a great debt to Dr Rainer Hildebrandt and his associates for maintaining the museum at Checkpoint Charlie and for their work in ensuring that we do not forget. Dieter Bergner not only gave us a lengthy interview

vi

but even played billiards for us – with spectacular results. Dr Heidemann of the German History Institute in London provided a balanced perspective of contemporary affairs for us, and Dorothea Sambas at the West German Embassy opened countless doors. Through them I gained access to many people both in Bonn and in Berlin. Of the former, I would especially mention Dr Joseph Dolezal, press spokesman for the Ministry of Inner German Affairs, and Detlof von Berg, of the West German Foreign Ministry.

In Berlin itself, Lothar Nass bothered untiringly about us and took on many of the arrangements. I would also like to mention with gratitude the help and advice I received from Stephen Laufer, Dr Dieter Senoner and Major James Miles. On a more personal level, I would like to thank Fred Warner for all his help, Beate Schubert, Margarete Spitzer, Horst Freimark, Phillip Warner, Peter Meyer, the Hewitt family, Major-General Rex Whitworth, Herr Krink, and Herr Müller who lent us a caravan.

Finally, my thanks must go to Petra Dombrowski of the Berlin office of the International Commission for Human Rights, and those associated with her, for opening my eyes to the realities. Beyond that it remains only to acknowledge the many Berliners who simply by talking to me, helped me to understand their particular problem. Certain of them I am not at liberty to name or otherwise identify.

I would have liked to have been able to include here a word of thanks to officials of the German Democratic Republic. In keeping with fair journalistic practices, we made a formal request for facilities to film on their side of the Wall and submitted a list of questions well in advance. If this book is perhaps one-sided, it is because our request was turned down after repeated telephone calls. This I regret, but I do not blame the officials with whom I had contact. Their hands were obviously tied from above.

Owing to an unforeseen illness, Caroline Marsh jumped in at the last minute to help me type the final manuscript, and I am humbly grateful for a Christmas spent at work.

A. K.

List of Illustrations

cellor Konrad Adenauer. The arches of the Gate were draped in red banners to stop East Germans from watching their visit.

21. Eighteen refugees escaped from East Berlin in this car.
22. This Isetta made several successful trips through the Wall.
23. The Austin-Healey Sprite used by Hans Peter Meixner.
24. Two successful escapes were made in this cable drum, which could carry four people. The third escape was betrayed.
25. Ilse Hewitt in East Berlin.
26. The driver of this bus tried to ram through the Wall unsuccessfully. Several of his passengers were hurt.
27. The Hewitts in London, after their escape.
28. Ilse and Philip Hewitt relive old memories in 1986.
29. Wolfgang Fuchs – heroic tunnel builder.
30. Wolf Quasner and Peter Meyer in 1986.
31. Wolf Quasner as a young man.
32. The extraordinary transformation of Peter Meyer.
33. Hanni safe in Berlin.
34. Peter safe in Berlin.
35. Bernauerstrasse today.
36. Memorials to just some of those who failed to escape.

Photographs are reproduced with thanks to the Checkpoint Charlie Museum and to Anthony Nutley at TVS.

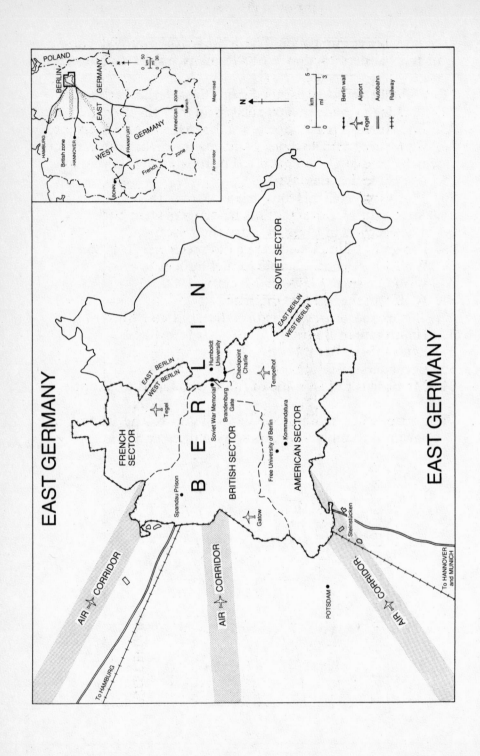

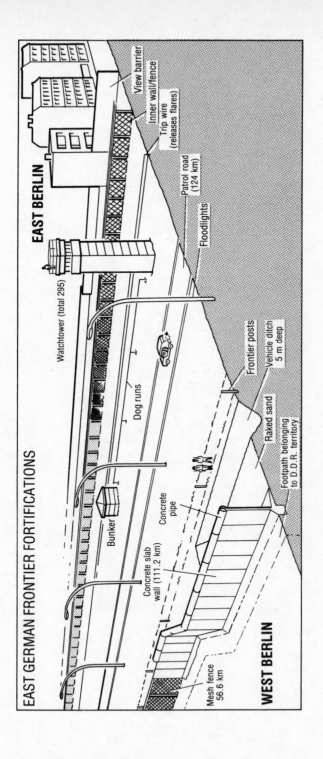

EAST GERMAN FRONTIER FORTIFICATIONS

EAST BERLIN

WEST BERLIN

Watchtower (total 295)

Dog runs

Bunker

Concrete pipe

Concrete slab wall (111.2 km)

Mesh fence 56.6 km

Footpath belonging to D.D.R. territory

Raked sand

Frontier posts

Vehicle ditch 5 m deep

Floodlights

Patrol road (124 km)

Trip wire (releases flares)

Inner wall/fence

View barrier

Introduction

Berlin is one of the perennial crisis zones that have tended to dog post-war history. Like Ulster, Vietnam and Afghanistan, it simply refuses to go away or be gracefully solved. It was once the capital of the Kaiser's Germany and was later destined to be transformed by the skill of Albert Speer into a fitting shrine for Hitler's thousand-year reich. Then the Allied bomber fleets intervened and spent several years attempting to obliterate this symbol of Prussian militarism, and what they left standing was finished off by the Red Army's artillery. Those same Allies, having managed to defeat the common enemy, found themselves occupying the ruins, and are still there today. The sad thing is that the generations that have grown up after the war, including the Germans themselves, have very little idea of the reason why. The fate of Austria was settled amicably and Germany, itself divided into two, has managed to settle down to peaceful co-existence. Yet, as a last vestige of four-power control, the divided city retains its special status, stuck in the middle of the German Democratic Republic. The latter regard their portion as their capital city although it is the Russian commandant who has the final say, dictated to him by his masters at the Kremlin. The Western part, consisting of the American, British and French sectors, is to all intents and purposes a monument to rampant consumerism. Its inhabitants tend to regard themselves as West Germans and govern themselves, but only within limits. The democratic process is hedged by the benign oligarchy of the three City

1

commandants. Berlin is above all a frontier city, where the superpowers meet eyeball to eyeball on a daily basis.

The political background and current status of Berlin have been adequately dealt with in numerous books, as has the history of the actual building of the Wall. The concern in the following pages is to explore the results of dividing a city in half in human terms, although enough general information to set the scene has been included. The Berlin Wall is unique and it is difficult to imagine comparative situations. There are other such borders, but they are generally designed to keep people out rather than stopping them from leaving. There is the border between China and Hong Kong, for instance, and the United States–Mexico frontier, which are guarded mainly to turn back hordes of immigrant workers who would otherwise threaten to swamp local economies. They are not, however, patrolled by whole regiments of troops with shoot-to-kill orders backed up by sophisticated fortifications. Neither do such borders arbitrarily divide a community which has been in existence for centuries, split families in half and meander through the streets of a once great city. Many countries have immigration restrictions which are laid down for social, economic or even racial reasons, but it would seem that only unelected Marxist governments find it necessary to wall in their own peoples. The DDR (German Democratic Republic) likes to describe itself as the Worker's Paradise, and has many solid achievements to its name, but the natural question is, if it is such a paradise, why are the workers not clamouring to be let in?

In discussing the Berlin situation it is easy to slip into the jargon of the Cold War, and when one reads the statistics of death on the border, to be consumed with righteous anger. One of the old jokes in West Germany is that the DDR is neither German nor democratic nor a republic, which to a large extent is true. It has even been described as the last bourgeois republic and its citizens as the last Prussians. A famous comment among the often obscene graffiti on the Wall reads – 'Will the last one out switch off the light'. The dream of an eventual reunification of Germany is a popular one, especially as many Germans have never managed to come to terms with the post-war division. The West Germans, and especially the

2

right-wing political parties, tend to regard themselves as the legitimate 'Germany' and in their newspapers they refer to the so-called DDR, or put the initials in inverted commas. The more extreme still refer to that country as the Soviet Occupation Zone, and anyone seeking some sort of political accommodation with the regime in the East is branded as a traitor. All this tends to foment a siege mentality on the part of the ruling clique in East Berlin and to confirm them in their belief that they are constantly threatened by West German neo-fascist, militarists and NATO warmongers. In their own jargon they refer to the 'anti-fascist protection wall' as if the frontier defences were to protect their own territorial integrity, rather than to stop their own people leaving. As they cannot go to the West, then where do they go? One imagines at least the possibility of free travel within the Socialist brother lands, but even this is not the case. Ever since Solidarity, Poland is more or less out of bounds, and to go to Russia they must join an organised 'cultural tour'. Yugoslavia is likewise banned, which leaves few alternatives. East Germans with whom the author has spoken, said that they felt unwelcome in Hungary and Bulgaria and were treated as second-class citizens by the locals, who were only interested in tourists with Western currency. As a result Czechoslovakia remains the most popular destination for a trip 'abroad'. One of the main motives of those who succeed in escaping is the desire to travel without hindrance.

Leaving the DDR is not easy, but there are ways. Occasionally in the West you will see a car with East German number plates and there are a considerable number of lorries on the autobahn. Freight drivers, for instance, have to prove their reliability and leave their families behind as hostages. The same applies to ordinary citizens who can under certain circumstances obtain permission to attend funerals or weddings in the West of immediate family members. They too can never cross the border as a complete family unit – the children must stay behind. For years now, East Germans can leave legally once they have reached pensionable age. As useless mouths to feed, the State lets them move to West Germany, which pays them their full pension rights and social security benefits –

because they are regarded not as foreigners but as Germans. In recent years, as a result of a slight thaw in relations between the two Germanys, is has been possible to apply to leave on account of 'bringing families together'. For example if an East German has parents living in the West, he can make an application, but its granting may well depend on his usefulness to the State. Others can make applications for exit visas but will then almost certainly find themselves subjected to chicanery and many have ended up in prison. Once in prison, however, they have another chance through being ransomed by the West German government. Bonn purchases political detainees for 40,000 DM per head, which is a valuable source of hard currency for the DDR authorities, who are thus tempted to stick people in prison. In recent years, some authorities have 'magnanimously' gone over to getting rid of their unwanted elements by depriving them of their citizenship and simply shoving them over the frontier. Among such lucky ones have been those who had applied to leave or had taken part in anti-government or 'peace' demonstrations, but included in the job lots have been habitual criminals and a number of future spies. Over 40,000 were simply expelled in 1984.

Those who do not fall into any of the above categories or who cannot wait to take their chance of leaving legally have only two courses open to them: to sit tight and dream, or to escape. This does not mean that every citizen of the DDR wishes to leave, but before the Wall, one in every nine did take the opportunity. There are many who have come to terms with the regime and are quite content. Others form part of the ruling elite or are Communist Party members and thus have a vested interest in the status quo. They have access to the various perquisites such as the ability to purchase Western goods in special shops. In addition, for every successful escape there are probably three attempts which have failed, to judge by the number of prisoners ransomed by the Bonn government. To take the analogy further, those who even get to the point of actually planning and carrying out an escape attempt are the active ones in the community. One thus wonders how many East Germans have toyed with the idea but have not had the necessary courage to risk their lives or to cut themselves off from a familiar environment.

This book deals with the whole history of escapes which in some ways have been connected with Berlin, but only a fraction of the total has been able to be included. In addition there are all the other escapes carried out by East Germans either over the border into West Germany or into other countries. The escapes themselves can be broadly divided into two categories. Firstly, there are those who have made their attempt completely off their own bat and without any form of outside assistance. Secondly, those people who have been assisted by one of the escape helping organisations, either from altruistic motives or for gain. Today, even on an 'expenses only' basis, the cost of flight from the East can be circa 100,000 DM which has to be found in Western currency either by the refugee himself or by relatives who are already living in the West. The risks involved are high. Seventy-five refugees are known to have died trying to cross the frontier in and around Berlin, but this total is almost certainly higher as it is based only on fatalities that are known to the authorities in the West. Hundreds more have been wounded and literally thousands have been caught and imprisoned. Yet still they try and every year a few succeed. In spite of Helsinki, shots are still fired along the Wall and the whole inhuman system seems to have a momentum of its own. The West Berliners may have learnt to live with the Wall and even to ignore it, but to those in the East its very existence is a reminder of their own impotence. Outside Berlin one might imagine that the West Berliners are walled in, but that is not really the case as they can leave at any time. It is their compatriots on the other side who are imprisoned as a result of the moral bankruptcy of the political system which rules them.

At the time of its 25th anniversary, politicians of all shades of opinion in the West pontificated about the Wall and speculated about its eventual demise. Pious sentiments were uttered about a gradual change in the climate of East-West relations and some sort of global settlement of the German question underwritten by the two superpowers. Yet all that is to ignore the realities. We all realise that any attempt to alter the status of

Berlin by either side would lead to war, and persistent claims by the DDR that the West German army is only waiting for a chance to march through the Brandenburg Gate with drums beating and colours flying is arrant nonsense. So what could negotiations achieve? The ruling elite in the East is not going to give up its privileged position, for the Party knows full well that free elections would have to be the prerequisite for a settlement. They would be booted out of office, as would any other East European regime for that matter. Perhaps they really do believe their own propaganda that the oppressed workers in the West will one day rise and throw off their capitalist masters. If they take down their own Wall, the population will once again vote with their feet, heading for the fleshpots of the West.

So, what about Berlin itself? The city is only 80 kilometres away from the Polish border at Frankfurt am Oder and is right in the middle of the territory of the DDR. You can reach the Western part by air along one of the recognised corridors, you can travel by train or you can drive along one of the authorised transit routes. If you choose the latter and happen to be a foreigner, you will have to pay five West marks for the privilege in the form of a transit visa. If you are a West German or West Berliner you go free, because the Bonn government pays an enormous sum to the DDR every year in lieu. Once in West Berlin you can cross over to the Eastern sector comparatively easily but must remain within the city boundary. For visits further into the DDR, you need a full visa, applied for in advance, plus pre-booked accommodation paid for in hard currency. The 'entry ticket' for a day trip to East Berlin costs five marks for the visa and you have to exchange twenty-five marks at the official one-to-one rate. If you are a foreigner, you must enter by car through Checkpoint Charlie or take the S-bahn train to Friedrichstrasse Station. West Germans have other entry points, but West Berliners have to apply two days in advance for a permit to cross the border. Just imagine that sort of rigmarole every time you wanted to visit your aunt or your grandmother.

As has already been mentioned, West Berlin is technically ruled by the three Allied commandants and is not part of the Federal Republic of Germany. The Allies meet in the Kommandantura building where there is always a spare chair at the table just in case the Russians decide to rejoin, and their flag flies outside along with the Stars and Stripes, the Union Jack and the Tricolour. Local government is in the hands of the Senate under the chairmanship of the Ruling Mayor, and politics tend to be dictated along the lines of the main West German parties, the Christian Democrats (CDU) and the Social Democrats (SPD). Berliners pay their taxes to Bonn and are ruled by West German law although they have no direct representation in the Bonn parliament – their members there have no voting rights and are nominated rather than being directly elected. In spite of that, West Berlin is to all intents and purposes a 'Land' or province of the Federal Republic, which every now and again holds a committee meeting in Berlin to prove a point – much to the fury of the DDR. The West German army has no presence or rights in Berlin and its citizens cannot be called up for military service.

The fiction of four-power government is maintained only in the Allied Air Safety Bureau which controls all air movements along the corridors to and from Berlin, and in the administration of the Spandau prison – whose only inmate is the lonely Rudolf Hess. Otherwise the only Russian presence in West Berlin is the permanent guard on their war memorial near the Brandenburg Gate, where they in turn are guarded by the British Army. The memorial is situated in a wired-in compound and only the tourist buses are allowed inside to cruise slowly past without allowing the passengers to disembark. Some years ago somebody took a pot shot at one of the Russians and as the memorial is in the British sector they are responsible for the security of the detachment. When the guard is changed, British military police escort the Russian convoy to and from the crossing point at the Invalidenstrasse.

West Berlin occupies an area of 480 square kilometres and has a population of nearly two million, yet there is no real sense of being hemmed in. You can pay a visit to the city and never even see the Wall, although this runs around the outside and straight through the centre. Nearly 16 per cent of the area is wooded and 7 per cent is used for agriculture and market gardening. There are rivers and lakes crowded with yachts in the summer, concert halls, Hitler's Olympic stadium, attractive parks and all the amenities of a major city. In spite of this the city is not self-sufficient and requires massive subsidies from Bonn to keep going. Bonn, however, needs Berlin for its symbolic value as the capital one day of a reunited Germany and the Western Allies must cling on to their toehold in the East if they are to maintain their credibility with the Germans and other NATO partners.

For their part, the East Germans would naturally like to swallow up West Berlin as its very presence right in the middle of their territory is a living reminder to their people of the validity of freedom. Western television and radio are constant reminders of the attractions of capitalist society and bring a little colour into otherwise drab lives. The only part of the DDR which cannot receive West German television programmes, for geographical reasons, is the area around Dresden – which is nicknamed 'the valley of the naïve'. It is said that government officials dread a transfer to Dresden as their wives and children complain about not being able to watch their favourite programmes.

The DDR realises that the Western part of the city cannot be taken over by force. Any attempt would reawaken massive sympathy and would lead to retaliation. There is strong evidence to suggest, however, that the East Germans hope to achieve their ends by destabilisation, slowly but steadily. As the frontier on the Eastern side is completely open and persons entering from the East are barely controlled, it is easy to infiltrate agents, drugs and seditious literature. To this has been added in recent years a stream of those seeking political asylum. Citizens from Third World countries have been flown in by Interflug, the East German airline, at knockdown prices and then simply pushed over the border into West Berlin. The authorities there have a responsibility under the constitution to cope and the vast numbers of foreigners have proved to be a burden on the city's coffers as well as fuelling racist propaganda. Add to this a perennial crop of political scandals, bribery and petty corruption among all parties in West Berlin, and it is no wonder that those in the East see their work being done for them.

In the chapters that follow, by no means all the escapes over, through or under the Wall are described. Many never receive any publicity at all and often those which are successful are kept quiet for fear that relatives in the East might suffer. Virtually all the people whose stories are featured came from quite ordinary backgrounds and, once in the West, settled down to perfectly normal unexciting lives. Regardless of their motives for escaping, which in many cases were economic rather than political, any person who has attempted to break out from East Germany has to have a great deal of courage. Not only do they have to pit themselves against the daunting technical fortifications but also against the problem of betrayal or denunciation. Planning an escape or encouraging someone else to escape is a crime. Those who wish to leave also face the opposition of the ranks of the Ministry for State Security, the *Volkspolizei* (known as *Vopos*) and the frontier police or *Grepos*. This book is dedicated to all those who dared and won and to those who tried and failed – the dead, the injured and the imprisoned.

THE BERLIN WALL – FACTS AND FIGURES

Total circumference	165.7km
Concrete wall	111.2km
Mesh fence	56.6km
Anti-tank obstacles	9.4km
Anti-vehicle ditch	198 km
Alarm signal wire	124 km
Patrol road (since 13.8.61)	124 km
Watchtowers	295
Bunkers	52
Dog runs	257
Incidents involving the use of firearms	1631
Bullet impacts in West Berlin	438
Use of firearms by West Berlin police	14
Arrests on the border	3130
Refugees (police figures)	4899
Refugees who were members of DDR armed forces or police	553
Deaths of refugees/escape helpers	75
Wounded by firearms	115
Attacks against the Wall	34

ARRIVALS IN WEST BERLIN 1985

Refugees	44
Those with visitors' permits who elected not to return	161
Ransomed political prisoners	904
Permitted to leave for family reunification	4054

1
Berlin – the City, the Stage

In comparison with most of the great cities of Europe, Berlin is a comparative adolescent, which in 1987 will be celebrating its 750th birthday. There will be two celebrations, reflecting the divided nature of the city, and each side is locked into bitter competition. 'Our festival will be more expensive, more splendid and more pompous than your festival.' As an adolescent, Berlin still has a certain pushiness and cockiness about it as if to emphasise its need to be taken seriously and be counted amongst grown-up cities. In order to understand Berlin and its present-day situation, it is necessary to make a short excursion into history and geography, while also having a brief look at some of the personalities who have left their mark on this most fascinating city.

Although the Berliners themselves would claim to be a part of Western Europe, it is worth remembering that the city is far closer to the present-day Polish border than to Western Germany. It grew up in the thirteenth century as a trading bridge between East and West – a market where merchants from the Germanic nation dealt in the goods from the Slavic world to the East. Two small towns, Berlin and Coelln, grew up in the latter part of the twelfth century on the River Spree, half way between the castles of Spandau and Koepenick, spanning a convenient ford. They were astride the ancient main road from Magdeburg to Posen (Poznan) and in the territory of the Margraves of Brandenburg. Until the 1440s, the townships were largely independent and self-governing during a chaotic

period of German history, but then a new family, the Hohenzollerns, gained the sovereignty over Brandenburg, one of the
Electorates which chose the Holy Roman Emperor. In 1448,
the proud merchant towns became the Electoral Residence of
Berlin/Coelln.

The presence of the Court led to a gradual increase in the
population and the construction of imposing monumental
buildings to house the Elector and his officials. But even more
important was the introduction of the Reformation in 1540
to Brandenburg, where Luther's doctrines found immediate
support. What is flippantly termed the 'Protestant work ethic'
proved to be the foundation of the expansionist dreams of the
Hohenzollerns and was to lead to the foundation of the Prussian
state. The Reformation led to the repeated occupation and
destruction of Berlin during the Thirty Years War. To make
good the loss in population, Frederick William, known as the
Great Elector, encouraged immigration. Louis XIV's edict
against the Protestant community in France brought an influx
of industrious families to Berlin, and by 1700 a fifth of the
inhabitants of the city were of French origin.

The Electors of Brandenburg ruled over considerable territories in the East along the Baltic coast, which formed the
Dukedom of Prussia (today split up between Poland and
Russia), and were outside the boundaries of the Empire. In
1701, the Elector Frederick had himself proclaimed King in
Prussia and laid down a significant cornerstone of the state that
during the eighteenth century was to expand from a minor
German power into being one of the arbiters of Europe. Much
of this was the responsibility of Frederick the Great, phil-
osopher, friend of Voltaire, musician, statesman and military
genius. He inherited a full treasury and a small but powerful
army from his father, and set out on a career of conquest.
Frederick added Silesia to his possessions in a series of wars,
and laid down a massive state bureaucracy, based on complete
obedience to the ruler.

Frederick ran Prussia with the precision of a martinet, controlled almost every aspect of its citizens' lives, and in the
process rebuilt Berlin into a worthy capital city of a small
nation that had become a European power. His successors, in

spite of having been humbled by Napoleon, continued to expand their territories, and to embellish their capital with impressive buildings to demonstrate their power. Industry flourished and burgeoned throughout the nineteenth century – textiles, porcelain, machinery and iron forging – all served by an ever-increasing railway network. This in turn led to a substantial increase in the population and the creation of an urban proletariat.

In January 1871, after the victory over France, Germany became an empire, united under the Prussian monarchy. Kaiser Wilhelm II transformed Berlin into a modern city on a par with many others in Europe. Museums, theatres and the arts experienced a renaissance during the years leading up to the First World War, yet in this period social tensions were beginning to undermine the foundations of the Kaiser's style of government. By 1912, the Social Democrats had 75 per cent of the votes in Berlin, and the Party as a whole was prepared to support the declaration of war two years later. But the First World War brought rationing and austerity and a radical change of attitude. In November 1918 the Communist revolution, which started with mutinies in the fleet at Kiel, reached Berlin. The Kaiser abdicated and a German republic was proclaimed under the leadership of a Social Democratic chancellor. The following years were chaotic as extremists to right and left struggled against the ill-defined republic. In the 1920s Germany very nearly became a Soviet-style communist state, and hyperinflation ruined many of the middle classes. No wonder that there was fertile ground for the insidious message of the National Socialists, who had arrived in Berlin from Bavaria. The Nazis never achieved a popular power base in socialist Berlin, but after Hitler's expulsion of the SDP members from the Reichstag (parliament), the city was ruled by Joseph Goebbels. As the capital of Hitler's Reich, Berlin was to be transformed into a symbol of Nazi achievement, but little of the architecture of that era remains. Throughout the war, the city was pounded day and night by fleets of Allied bombers, though it still continued to function. Thousands of civilians were killed and whole residential areas were obliterated as the citizens moved into the cellars and shelters. On 2

May 1945, Berlin capitulated to the Russians, but the victors marched into a ghost city. Those who had survived crawled out into a lunar landscape of rubble, and were subjected to an orgy of rape and plunder before the Russians managed to get their troops under control. There was no gas, no electricity and no water. The SS had blown up the underground railway tunnels under the Spree river and the system was flooded. One-fifth of all buildings were ruined or could no longer be restored. Ration cards were given out but there was little in the way of food to be had. The wealthy exchanged valuable antiques and jewellery for potatoes and flour, while the poor went hungry. Those who survived that period will never forget the privations, but Berliners have always been tough. They never lost their sense of humour.

The fate of Berlin and its citizens had been decided by the British, Americans and Russians at two meetings well before the war ended (the French were included among the victors only after the end of hostilities). The Foreign Ministers' Conference in Moscow in 1943 occupied itself with the problem of what to do with a defeated Germany and the participants decided to set up a body known as the European Advisory Commission, based in London, to come up with proposals. The Allies wanted unconditional surrender which naturally assumed that they would have to take over the government, but there was no intention of dismembering the country or forming separate states. The consensus was to divide Germany into zones of occupation, at first three and then four, to include France. This left Berlin slap in the middle of the Russian zone. It was decided that Berlin would have to have some form of special status. The proposed organ of government for the whole country was to be the Allied Control Commission which needed to be located on territory common to all the victor nations. In addition, Berlin had great symbolic value and everyone wanted to have a presence there, regardless of who captured it.

So it was decided by the terms of the London Protocol in November 1944 that each of the Allies would have a sector in Berlin and that the entire city would be governed by the various commandants meeting in the Kommandantura. Under them would be an executive composed of 'suitable' Germans, the Magistrat. It was quite clear that no part of greater Berlin was part of the Russian zone then or at any time, and the Russians placed their signature under the London agreements. The sectors of the city were divided up on the basis of the boundaries of the traditional boroughs.

The argument as to whether the Western Allies should have advanced beyond the Elbe and captured Berlin is unimportant here. The Russians got to Berlin first, and it was not until the beginning of July that the British and Americans were able to march in and claim their sectors – the French arrived in August. The remaining problem which had been left open was that of right of access. The Western powers had always assumed the goodwill of Soviet Russia in making the occupation work. Only the basic air corridors had been agreed in writing. As far as road and rail links were concerned, as the zones were regarded as provisional solutions and not as embryo states, it was simply assumed that since the Western powers had the right to be in Berlin they also had the right to travel there. They had no indication that the transit routes would later be used to pressurise them into leaving.

All the Allies were in agreement that National Socialism had to be destroyed root and branch, but they differed as to how this was to be done. The Russians made a start even before the other Allies arrived in Berlin, by establishing a Magistrat, half the members of which were Communists and who took over key administrative positions. Many of them had been in exile in Moscow and had returned behind the bayonets of the Red Army. In June 1945 the Russians permitted the reforming of political parties in their zone and in Berlin – Christian Democrats, Liberals, Social Democrats and Communists. The intention of the latter was to rebuild Germany on Soviet principles, and, under Russian pressure, the Social Democrats were persuaded to join with them to form the Social Unity Party (SED) in April 1946 – the same entity which today rules the DDR. In the Russian sector there was no vote, but in the Western sectors, in a free election, more than 80 per cent of Social Democrats rejected the proposal. Only the presence of the Western Allies had made such an example of the democratic

15

process possible. From then on the sector borders tended more and more to assume the character of political lines of demarcation. In October of that year, the first and last free elections in Greater Berlin were held, resulting in a disaster for the Communists, who only managed to win 19.8 per cent of the votes cast, and a victory for the Social Democrats, who formed a majority in the city administration. In June 1947, the Russians vetoed the appointment of the Social Democrat, Ernst Reuter, as governing mayor, and the Western Powers gave way, still trying to maintain the fiction of Allied unity. But as the Cold War increased in intensity, unity proved an illusion.

As a result of the Second World War, Soviet power expanded from the Adriatic, via the Elbe to the Baltic and, wherever Soviet armies marched in, puppet regimes were installed. The contrast between Soviet-style communism and Western democracy had been papered over during the war by the need to defeat the Nazis, but after the euphoria of victory had ebbed away, it became more obvious that there was no common ground. Until 1949, the United States had a monopoly on nuclear weapons by which Russia felt threatened. The Americans began to realise that their erstwhile allies intended to swallow up Europe. To provide a bulwark against the attractions of communism, the Americans and the other Western powers decided to rebuild the economies of their zones and turn the defeated Germans into partners. The decision was made in February 1948, and shortly afterwards the Russians left the Control Commission, effectively ending the four-power government of Germany. The four powers had been trying to negotiate a currency reform in order to provide a sound basis for economic recovery, but had failed to reach agreement. Therefore Britain, France and America introduced the D-Mark into their zones in the West on 20 June 1948, and two days later the Russians took a similar step. In Berlin they tried to introduce the Ost-Mark through the city, in order to capture the economy. But the Western powers countered by establishing the D-Mark in their sectors – thus coupling their economies more closely with the Western zones. By this time the Russians realised that West Berlin had become an irritating foreign body in the middle of their own backyard, and decided to try to eliminate it.

The chosen method was to attempt to starve out the city, which up until then had been largely supplied from the West. Using the excuse of 'technical difficulties', they cut the road and rail links leading into the city on 24 June 1948. There remained two possibilities: to force a way through by armed force, which could well have led to war, or to use the air corridors, which the Russians had not considered. The American military governor in Germany was the tough General Lucius Clay, and the West Berliners were led by the courageous Ernst Reuter. He inspired the citizens to take on the challenge and to accept privation in return for their freedom, while the British and Americans got down to the problem of supplying a city of two million inhabitants by air. At the start, the food stocks were only enough for 36 days and coal for 45 days. The Russians cut power supplies from their sector into the Western sectors and in Berlin, the lights went out.

The ten-month air lift was one of the most inspiring post-war achievements, both from a technical point of view and with regard to its long-term political effect. It demonstrated to the Berliners that the Allies' eyes had been finally opened to the Russian menace and that they were determined to hold on to the city. The privations united the inhabitants and the majority turned down the tempting offers of food from the East. Their courage brought them the sympathy of the free world and did much to convince that world that Germany could once again be trusted. Aircraft were brought together from all over Europe and old bombers were converted into transport planes. The basic daily need for the city was 12,000 tons of supplies. At the beginning only 120 tons could be transported. After a few weeks Britain and America had upped this to 4000 tons, and on one day the following April, the record daily delivery was almost 13,000 tons. They even managed to fly in coal and a power station broken down into components – which is still working today. Round the clock, day in and day out, the aircraft were landing at one-and-a-half minute intervals at Gatow and Tempelhof airfields. Later, using rubble from bombed buildings, the Berliners built Tegel airport in the French zone.

Around the turn of the year 1948/49, the Russians began to realise that they had lost their gamble and that their international reputation had sunk drastically, while the Western countries were united as never before. The occupiers had become the protectors and friends. During the blockade, the Magistrat and the city parliament had continued to hold their meetings in the East, but had been disturbed by violent Communist demonstrations designed to put them under pressure. The democratic parties saw themselves forced to hold their sittings in the West, and after the Communists had reformed the Magistrat by packing it with their followers, the freely elected members also moved to the West on 1 December 1948. The proposed elections could only be held in the Western sectors and as a result, Ernst Reuter was confirmed as governing mayor. In May 1949 the Federal Republic of Germany was formally recognised as the sovereign state founded from the three Western zones, and the Russians finally lifted the blockade. They formed their zone into the German Democratic Republic (DDR) the following October, and that state's administration set itself up in East Berlin which became its capital. As far as the Western powers were concerned, their sectors were economically and legally connected to the Federal Republic, but did not become a part of it. The Allies continued to meet in the rump Control Commission and to oversee the affairs of West Berlin.

During the 1950s West Berlin became more and more isolated as the authorities in the East kept up the pressure. Tram and bus connections were cut, leaving only the S-bahn railway system and the Underground still running. West Berliners, although able to move freely into East Berlin, were prohibited from visiting the DDR without special permission and were subjected to constant chicanery on the transit routes. The cleft between the two Germanys was deepened even further when the Federal Republic joined NATO in 1955 and the DDR became a member of the Warsaw Pact. Bonn, however, continued to maintain that the situation was only a temporary one and that Germany would be reunited with its capital in Berlin. The Federal Republic has always maintained that citizens of the DDR are German citizens and accords them equal rights.

18

1. An East German soldier erecting a barbed wire barricade – the beginning of the Wall.

2. A working party stringing wire across a Berlin street in August 1961.

3. One of the early escapes – through barbed wire.

4. *The face of freedom. A happy couple arrive in West Berlin in August 1961.*

5. *American tanks at Checkpoint Charlie in October 1961.*

6. *Confrontation October 1961. An American staff car escorted by jeeps leaves the East Zone at Checkpoint Charlie.*

German industriousness in the West of the city, fired by American loans and West German support, rebuilt the city steadily. The old city centre remained in the East, so new government buildings had to be created and a new shopping centre grew up around the Kurfurstendamm. East Berliners could still cross relatively freely into the West, where they could read newspapers and visit the cinema. Considerable numbers worked in the West and were paid in D-Marks which they spent on goods unobtainable in their own sector. All this represented a running sore to a regime which had to rely on manipulation of the media to claim legitimacy, and which resorted to terror to keep its inhabitants in check. The DDR was economically exploited by its Russian masters, and as the cupboard became barer so the people turned to the West as a source of inspiration. Sooner or later, the sore would have to be eliminated or the very existence of the DDR would be at stake.

2

The Building of the Wall

If there was any one event that was to lead directly to the decision to build the Wall, it was the workers' revolt in East Germany on 17 July 1953. A year earlier the SED Party Congress had decided that the build-up of socialism had to be consolidated, and among other decisions it was agreed to collectivise the farmers on a 'voluntary' basis and to dispossess the many independent artisans and small businesses. By the following spring the supply of food to the population had begun to break down and the concentration on heavy industry at the expense of consumer goods led to much popular discontent. Farmers had fled in droves to West Germany to avoid the effects of collectivisation and the new farms were totally mismanaged. Industrialists and shopkeepers began to join in the growing resistance by voting with their feet. Joseph Stalin died on 5 March, but the new masters in the Kremlin were in no mood to help the East Germans out of the mess that they had got themselves into. However, instead of drawing the inevitable conclusions the SED leadership decided at the end of May to increase the norms for industrial workers by 10 per cent. In the background, there was a deep division within the Party, with one faction opting for a relaxation of the drive for socialism. The Party Secretary, Walther Ulbricht, and his faction were determined to push their proposals through, including the norm increases. On 16 July the building workers in East Berlin went on strike and demanded a return to the previous norms – which they could easily exceed and thereby earn valuable bonuses. During the afternoon a demonstration started which soon had 10,000 workers on the streets marching to the government offices. It became clear that they were not just demanding a reduction in norms, as voices began to demand the resignation of the government and free elections. On the morning of 17 July, a virtual general strike had broken out all over the DDR. Flags were pulled down, party offices were plundered and political prisoners liberated, but by the afternoon Soviet troops and the *Volkspolizei* (*Vopos*) regained control of the situation. More than three hundred died and over a thousand were injured. Those who had hung on and hoped for improvement were forced to realise that the Russians had backed Ulbricht and that the Western powers would not risk a war to help them.

One direct result was a great increase in the numbers of refugees crossing the still relatively open frontier between the two Germanys, which in turn led to the decision in May 1952 to fortify the zonal border between the DDR and the Federal Republic. Those who lived directly on the border had to obtain special permission to remain, and 'undesirable' elements were forcibly moved well into the interior. Fortifications, wire, watchtowers and minefields grew apace all along the border, leaving Berlin as the only relatively easy crossing place.

In November 1958, Khrushchev demanded that the Western powers give up the remnants of their occupation rights in Berlin, in order to 'normalise' the situation. They should withdraw their troops, in return for which the whole of Berlin would be turned into a free state. If they did not agree, Russia would make a separate agreement with the DDR and transfer to them the right as a sovereign state to control the transit routes – including the air corridors. He set a six-month ultimatum for agreement, which was rejected. The Western Allies realised that if Berlin was lost, the rest of free Europe could well follow. The Berlin crisis dragged on into 1959 and 1960 when the four powers negotiated without success at Geneva. In Vienna in July 1961 President Kennedy laid down 3 principles governing Western thinking:

The defence of the Western presence

> Maintenance of the right of free access
> Maintenance of the right of the West Berliners to self-deter-
> mination of their way of life

The Vienna summit broke down and President Kennedy returned to the USA with Russian threats ringing in his ears. His government increased its defence budget and began to plan for armed intervention in Berlin. The Allied secret services were of the opinion that Ulbricht would put a defended frontier between East Berlin and the rest of the DDR.

Back in Germany refugees were leaving the DDR at an alarming rate. In 1960 a total of 200,000 people left, 75 per cent via Berlin. In July 1961 30,000 left in one month, many of whom were skilled workers and professional people. Throughout those summer months up to 2000 refugees were pouring every day into the emergency reception centres in West Berlin. In the East the State tried to stop the flood. The authorities blamed Western capitalist firms for enticing their peaceful citizens into leaving the republic. They imprisoned those who they managed to stop. The plain fact was that the DDR was slowly but surely being strangled economically, as the harvest lay uncollected in the fields and the state factories could no longer deliver punctually. As the economic miracle in West Germany reached its zenith, the factories there were desperately short of skilled labour, and where better to recruit than in the East, where there was no language problem? An added complication was caused by the 53,000 East Berliners who crossed over to the West to work every day, the so-called *grenzgänger* (border-crossers). They were paid in Western currency which they could illegally exchange for East-marks at a rate of one to four, while enjoying the cheap rents in the Eastern part of the city.

In the summer of 1961 there was an air of crisis hanging over Berlin and the threat of war was a real one. The Western powers, however, their policy based on the nuclear deterrent, were not equipped to fight a local limited action in defence of their rights in Berlin. The Allied garrisons amounted to a weak division, 150 miles away from their nearest support units in West Germany which would have to fight their way through

to the city. Their opposition would have consisted of 26 divisions in the DDR with a further 50 Warsaw Pact divisions
within easy reach. Berlin itself, after the bitter experience of
the blockade, had been stocked with enough food to last the
population of the Western sectors for a year. The politicians
in West Germany were busy with an election campaign, and
the cosmonaut Titov was circling the earth in a space capsule.
In Moscow there was a summit meeting of Warsaw Pact leaders
at the beginning of August, at which Ulbricht was given the
go ahead to take steps to halt the flood of refugees. Rumours
began to spread throughout the DDR of some sort of impend-
ing action, which only served to increase the numbers fleeing
over the border. Orders had been issued that all those working
in the West must register with the authorities, that from 1
August they would have to pay for their rent and utilities in
West-marks and by the end of September to take jobs in the
DDR. Many saw the writing on the wall and left. In addition,
army and police units took up positions on the roads and
at railway stations leading into Berlin, stopping anyone with
luggage or without a valid reason for entering the city limits.

In July, in reply to a question put by a journalist, Ulbricht
had said 'nobody has any intention of building a wall', but on
9 August he called together his inner cabinet for a meeting
at his country house, where the decision was taken. Erich
Honecker, Secretary for National Security, was put in charge
of a specially formed staff which moved into the East Berlin
police headquarters. Direct telephone lines to army units and
the Russians were installed, as orders for a general alert were
issued. By the evening of 11 August the necessary plans had
been worked out and every roll of barbed wire in the country
had been requisitioned. Many of the refugees who arrived that
day commented on the large numbers of military vehicles that
were on the roads and moving into the city. As for the West
Berliners, many of them took advantage of the warm summer
weekend to go swimming in the Wannsee or for walks in the
Grunewald. On the Saturday night, some 20,000 troops of the
New Peoples' Army and 4000 members of the *Kampfgruppen*,
the Party militia, opened their sealed orders to discover that
their destination was Berlin.

Just before 2 o'clock on the Sunday morning the powerful floodlights at the Brandenburg gate were switched off, and in the darkness the few passers-by noticed the shapes of lorries and armoured cars on the Eastern side. Shadowy figures of men were unloading things from the lorries, and it was the same story at the Potsdamerplatz and in the Bernauerstrasse. Throughout East Berlin other armed units were closing and padlocking the entrances to the Underground and S-bahn stations on all the lines leading into the West. Many late-night revellers found themselves having to walk home, witnessing the fact that coils of barbed wire were being laid across all the sector crossing points and workers with pneumatic drills were starting to dig up the roadways. The first report to be received in the West was from United Press International, timed at 03.25 hours: 'Strong units of the Communist Peoples' Police have blocked off the sector border between East and West Berlin during the course of the night.' By dawn it was discovered that of the 95 streets that had previously connected the two parts of the city, all except 13 had been barricaded, and those remaining open were guarded by armed police units, who were also guarding the bridges over the canals. While Berlin slept, families were divided, loving couples were separated and an entire community was disrupted.

As journalists hastened to find out what was going on, the politicians took their time. Chancellor Adenauer was wakened but went back to sleep again, and his opponent in the election campaign, Berlin's ruling mayor, Willi Brandt, was asleep on a train in West Germany. President de Gaulle was in the country for the weekend, and the British Prime Minister, Harold Macmillan, was in Scotland grouse shooting. The Foreign Minister, Sir Alec Douglas-Home, was likewise occupied, and neither of them saw any reason to return to London. In Washington, Kennedy determined that as none of the three principles had been infringed, he would wait to see what happened. This was despite the fact that the presence of DDR army units in the city was in direct contravention of the occupation agreements.

An official in West Berlin managed to contact the station master at a small station near Kassel and asked him to stop the

Nuremberg to Kiel express and ask Herr Brandt to return to Berlin immediately. This was done and the ruling mayor left the train at Hannover and took the first aircraft to Berlin. From the airport he has driven to the Brandenburg Gate where he saw the East German troops at work and the first of his fellow citizens who were gathering there. Just as Ulbricht was restricted by his Russian masters, so Brandt's hands were tied by the Allied city commandants. He met with them that afternoon without result, although he demanded action. They said that there was little they could do without authority from their political masters, who were difficult to reach on a Sunday. During the course of the morning there were sad scenes as relatives waved to each other across the wire and shouted messages. More and more people were gathering to hurl insults at the East German guards and during the afternoon thousands had assembled at the Brandenburg Gate. Soon stones began to fly as the crowd surged forward and the East replied with a water cannon and teargas. The West Berlin police were faced with the unwelcome task of forcing their own fellow citizens back. Everywhere there was a feeling of frustrated rage and powerlessness. Soon there were shouts of 'where are the Allies'?

On the following morning, Monday 14 August, Berlin awoke to clouds and drizzle. All along the wired-off frontier, the small businesses that had lived off trade with East Berlin waited in vain for their first customers. The lecture halls at the University were half-empty and in countless firms key workers and management staff were missing. During the afternoon there were spontaneous strikes and 6000 people assembled in front of the Schöneberger Rathaus, seat of the West Berlin government. Many wondered when Adenauer would put in an appearance, but he preferred to continue his election campaign, using the occasion of a speech in Regensburg to launch a personal attack on Brandt. All the latter could do was to ask the demonstrators to remain disciplined and keep the peace. His only weapon was a loudspeaker van which cruised up and down the border broadcasting slogans into the East.

Outside Berlin, the propaganda war was joined with a vengeance as the Western nations attacked the building of the Wall as a declaration of moral poverty on the part of communism.

For their part the East Germans were forced on the defensive as they tried to justify their 'new peace frontier', which later became the 'anti-fascist protection wall'. They claimed that NATO manoeuvres had threatened their territory and that German capitalists and warmongers were planning to commit armed aggression against the peace-loving peoples of the DDR. In the city itself, the anti-American feeling of the demonstrators increased, and German politicians demanded some sort of action, which was not forthcoming. The Americans remained cool and detached, justifying their attitude that their rights had not been infringed – only the Eastern sector was affected, for which they were not responsible. All that happened was that a mild protest was sent to the Russians by the US government. That evening Adenauer, together with his foreign minister, appeared on television in Bonn, where both uttered platitudes and warned against panic. They were partly justified in their warning as some West Berliners had flooded into airline offices and made enquiries about furniture removals. At the Marienfelde refugee reception centre, staff were finally able to take a break after the months of work around the clock to feed, clothe and register the daily influx of new arrivals from the East.

Three days after the forced division of the city, on the afternoon of 16 August, thousands of demonstrators once again assembled in front of the Schöneberger Rathaus, egged on by anti-American headlines in the morning papers and remarks about Macmillan having gone shooting. The mob chanted: 'We need protection, where are the protectors?' and 'Paper protests don't stop tanks'. In the middle of the afternoon, in pouring rain, 20,000 people had gathered on the square in front of the Rathaus, and at 4 o'clock Willi Brandt stepped out onto the front to speak to them. That morning he had written a polite but sharp letter to Kennedy, demanding support, and was in no mood to mince his words. To thunderous applause, the mayor attacked the Russians and their puppets in the East, and also demanded that the Western powers do something to recover their lost prestige. 'Berlin expects more than words. Berlin expects political action.' In the meanwhile, in Washington, Kennedy had received Brandt's letter and was angered by its tone. His initial reaction was to ignore it.

The following morning, however, he had to change his mind as he was made aware of the bitter anti-American feeling in West Berlin. After lengthy discussions it was decided to increase symbolically the US garrison by 1500 men and to send a high-level delegation to the city. This was to be led by Vice-President Johnson and the still popular post-war military governor, General Clay. Johnson had no particular desire to go to Berlin, but his visit was a tremendous success. He arrived at Tempelhof during the afternoon of 19 August to a tumultous welcome and was driven to the Rathaus through packed streets. He and Clay were bombarded with flowers and the Vice-President hopped out of the car frequently to shake hands. He spoke to a crowd similar in size to that which only a few days earlier had insulted America, and managed completely to restore the morale of the Berliners. The following day he took the salute as 1500 GIs rolled into West Berlin as the promised reinforcements for the garrison. Johnson made it quite clear that they were not going to tear down the Wall, but that America would honour her guarantees to the Western sectors.

So the Wall became a fact of life. During the 1960s Walther Ulbricht managed to save his economy and build the DDR into the most powerful of the satellite states. The Russians were also content and quietly let their other demands drop. There was no more talk of a separate peace treaty with the DDR. Everyone began to learn to live with the wall, and a few began to think about escape.

3

The Early Escapes

The social consequences of the decision to build the Berlin Wall were immense. Families who previously lived in different sectors of the city but had been able to visit regularly were separated by the latest manifestation of the Iron Curtain. Cross-sector romances were brought to an abrupt end, children could no longer visit their grandparents, aunts and uncles. Weddings, christenings and even funerals in the West or East had to be celebrated without the participation of family members who happened to live on the wrong side of the border. A young girl who had been brought up in the borough of Prenzlauerberg had fallen in love with a young man from Wedding and had married him, but could no longer pop over on Sunday for coffee and cakes with her mother and father. Yet quite possibly from the window of her apartment she could see the flat where she had been born and the streets where she had played as a child. The family tragedies were the obvious results, but it is worth considering the economic consequences as well. Workers from East Berlin had provided much of the manpower for the industry of West Berlin, forming a reliable pool of docile and inexpensive labour. They were sorely missed in the factories and workers from Western Germany were hard to find in spite of tax incentives to persuade them to move to the divided city. The answer was to recruit *gastarbeiter*, foreign labour from Southern Europe, which has led to the largest concentration of Turks outside Turkey. The borough of Kreuzberg is known locally as 'little Ankara' with all that that can imply in the way of racial and religious tension. In the years after 1961 Berlin suffered an economic decline owing to the relatively high costs of shipping industrial products through the DDR into the West, and even today, the city is only really kept afloat through massive subsidies from the Bonn government.

The seeming hopelessness of the situation after the building of the Wall resulted in a steady decline in the population as young people moved away to start new lives in the less restricted atmosphere of Western Germany. They tended to be replaced, however, by young West Germans who moved to Berlin to avoid compulsory military service. Under the Allied occupation status, West German armed forces have no presence in Berlin and thus Berliners cannot be called up. Many of these new citizens tended to be left-wing which perhaps explains the radical nature of student politics in the divided city. The old, however, have tended to stay with their roots. A visitor to Berlin cannot fail to remark on the comparatively high proportion of the elderly in the streets or to notice the advertisements for firms of undertakers on almost every bus stop and street corner heading.

Rome was not built in a day and neither was the Berlin Wall. We have seen that during the first few days, only limited strands of barbed wire were emplaced and sections of main crossing roads torn up. By the middle of September, however, 3 kilometres of primitive concrete wall had been erected, consisting of roughly cemented breeze blocks. By the end of 1961 many of the houses directly on the Eastern side of the frontier had been demolished and 130 watchtowers had been set up. Work was started on emplacing obstacles in the rivers and canals. Even after five years there were only 25 kilometres of Wall, the rest of the border being still defended by barbed wire. The number of watchtowers, however, had risen to 210, and in many places vicious dogs were tethered in the death strip, able to run along parallel to the border on taut cables. In addition, bunkers were sunk into the ground to supplement the towers.

As soon as the awful truth sank in, people on both sides of the artificial border began to plan escapes. The main impetus was naturally for family reasons, and during the first few days it was still comparatively easy to get across. West Germans could travel freely into East Berlin with day passes which were relatively easy to forge and cars were seldom searched very thoroughly. Ominously, however, the first shots were fired and the first people died. Since that Sunday in August 1961, seventy-five are known to have been killed, although the total is probably considerably higher.

On the Monday morning several thousand refugees from the East had registered at the Marienfelde reception centre, but many of those had been in the Western sectors quite legitimately for the weekend and had simply elected not to return home. Officially, twenty-eight refugees had crossed on the Sunday night and early Monday morning. A family of three swam the Teltow Canal, and one man managed to scramble through the primitive chicken wire barricade erected behind the ruins of the Reichs Chancellery building.

During the afternoon there was a dramatic incident in Reinickendorf. A young East Berliner ran over the railway tracks alongside the Kopenhagener Strasse heading west and pursued by three *Vopos*. They caught him and threw him to the ground, starting to question him as he lay in the middle of the railway line. Suddenly he struggled free and grabbed the rifle of one of the policemen, with which he was able to threaten them. Then, still holding the rifle, he started to run again towards the demarcation line only 30 metres away. He had actually reached West Berlin territory when his pursuers caught up once again and a struggle ensued, in the course of which the refugee was wounded in the knee by a bayonet. Screaming, he fell to the ground and the three policemen retreated to their own side of the border. The injured man, unable to walk, crawled to a nearby allotment colony crying out for help and was taken away to hospital.

At about the same time, Kurt Wismar was sitting in his flat in Kopenick, realising that it was a case of then or never. Three days earlier, in an act of foolhardy bravery, he had stood up during a meeting at the factory where he worked which was being visited by Walter Ulbricht, and had loudly demanded free elections. As a result he had been interrogated by the works committee and ever since had been shadowed by two State Security men in plain clothes. When he had returned from night shift early on the Sunday morning, the two had grinned at him as if to say – 'you won't get away from us now'. Not having listened to the radio, he had gone to bed. When he got up he looked out of the window and discovered that the two guardians were no longer there. He mentioned the fact to his fiancée, Helga, who had just come out of the kitchen and it was she who told him that the frontier had been sealed off. She said: 'they have better things to do now than keep an eye on you'. At lunch, he discussed the situation with Helga and the two of them decided that they had to get away that day. His outburst at the factory had made him a marked man.

All afternoon they listened to Western radio and watched West Berlin television, seeing the pictures of the *Volksarmee* stretching the coils of barbed wire, inserting posts and digging up the streets. This made Kurt decide that their best chance was to swim, in the hope that the authorities had not had time to get around to the canals and rivers. That evening, after Helga had slipped outside to check that the State Security men really had disappeared and were not simply hiding around the corner, the couple went out when it started to get dark. Acting as young lovers they wandered off to the local S-bahn station and travelled into the city centre. He was dressed in raincoat, a pullover and tracksuit bottom, while she was wearing a light-coloured summer costume. In her handbag were their personal papers and part of Kurt's precious stamp collection.

Their first approach was to the Warsaw Bridge and then along to the Oberbaum Bridge, as they had heard that these might still be open, but they were stopped by soldiers and factory militiamen who were all over the place. Still trying to act as a couple out for a stroll they turned down into the Stralauerstrasse which runs alongside the Spree and some barge docks. Kurt said: 'my fiancée and I were nervous and she was trembling. I still had no idea where and how we were going to get across.' As they walked they encountered two *Vopos* on patrol and as they passed by, one of the men half-turned towards them. Kurt broke into a cold sweat when he recognised the man as his local copper from Kopenick: 'who knew all about the business with Ulbricht and that I was on the black list.' But as luck would have it he was wrong, the policemen were so deep in conversation that they did not recognise their errant neighbour.

By then it was close to midnight and the young couple took the last S-bahn train to Treplau Park. There they found the border was lined with fresh barbed wire and lit up by large arc lights. Kurt's idea was to reach the bridge over the Landwehr Canal, but a short distance before the bridge there was a police control point where they were checking identity cards. Foiled there, Kurt and Helga then turned into an army camp, and smelt the soup being cooked in a field kitchen. Outside were sentries checking the papers of all passers-by. Kurt and Helga could see that the entrance to the Warsaw Bridge was blocked off by a wooden fence, but then he noticed that there were new blocks of flats beside the bridge and on the other side of them was the Landwehr Canal. He said to Helga: 'come on. Let's go over there and act as if we live in the new houses.' This they did without attracting attention and hid themselves in the bushes that grew on a patch of waste ground. As they heard no shouts they then climbed over a heap of rubble and down to the canal bank. It was a clear moonlit night and a few lights were reflected on the still waters of the canal. In the distance they could see sentries on the bridge and both admitted afterwards that at that stage they were scared stiff. But only a 25-metre swim and then they would be in safety.

Kurt and Helga undressed down to their underclothes, and wrapped their possessions in the raincoat. Then slipping from the covering bushes they were in the water. 'It wasn't cold. We managed to slide in without making any waves and swam very slowly. I was worried on the way that if the slightest thing happened, my fiancée would panic and get into difficulties. I said to her, "slowly, little one, we are going to make it".' Kurt was swimming with one hand, while in the other he grasped the precious handbag full of stamps. Then all of a sudden he felt something solid under his feet, the stonework of the far bank, which was so slippery that they fell back a couple of times before getting ashore. There they found themselves in an allotment colony and took shelter as they were both almost naked. The problem was that their clothes were still on the other side wrapped up in the raincoat. As there was no sign of excitement where they had come from, Kurt decided to swim back and collect their things, telling Helga to call out quietly if she saw danger. Stealthily he swam back, grasped the bundle and was on his return trip when he heard her call out: 'take care, there are *Vopos* coming.' 'I turned on my back and in the moonlight saw two men with rifles moving out from behind the shadow of a tree about a hundred metres away from me. They ran towards the place I had just left. Without bothering any more about noise I swam the last few metres and threw myself on land'. Once there Kurt wounded his leg on some barbed wire and felt the blood trickling down. On the other side he could see the *Vopos* running up and down but they made no effort to follow him and eventually made off. 'Probably they didn't even report it. They had been snoozing behind the tree as we swam off the first time, otherwise they certainly would have seen us.'

Kurt told Helga that they were in Neukolln, as she still could not really believe that they were in the West, and they made their way through the allotments towards a newly built block of flats. 'We looked like pigs, half naked, wet, dirty and me with blood pouring down my leg. I said to my fiancée "You stay here and I'll go for help".' Kurt ran towards the entrance of the block and pressed the bells one after the other, but nobody answered. Then he saw a light on the other side of the road, coming from a pub. After Kurt's banging on the locked door, the landlord opened up at last. Standing there dripping in his underpants, Kurt politely said: 'please excuse me for disturbing you so late but I've just come from over there.' The landlord did not seem particularly surprised. He said, 'don't stand there talking, lad. You'll freeze. You're the third today.' Then he poured out a cognac and called an ambulance. When this arrived, Kurt told the driver that they had to look for his fiancée – she was in the allotments and had no clothes on. They went to the gardens but it was only when she heard Kurt's voice that she emerged from hiding, shivering with cold and clad only in bra and pants.

The figure for the Monday night was quoted as: forty-one.

Another couple swimming the Teltow Canal were fired at by border guards. who luckily missed. By the Wednesday, searchlights and machine guns were installed there, and patrol boats cruised along many other stretches of waterway. Workmen were moved into the sewers and the entrances to underground stations were blocked off by bricks and mortar.

A focus of many of the early escape attempts was the Bernauerstrasse where the front doors of the houses led directly on to the pavement which was in the French sector. By the Wednesday, the inhabitants of the ground-floor flats were required to hand over their front door keys to the police after several of them had simply walked away to freedom. Other *Vopos* were stationed in the corridors to guard against further attempts. One man was caught trying to smuggle the wife of a friend out through his house at No. 47 and was arrested. Through an oversight he was released, and wasting no time he used a spare key that he had retained to let himself and his family out through the locked front door. The following day, guards began to swarm into the buildings together with workmen whose job it was to brick up all the windows facing towards the West. Those still living there shouted out to Western passers-by and began to climb out and drop onto the pavement. Soon West Berlin police and the fire brigade arrived with a net into which people could jump. Many made it under the eyes of newsmen and camera crews, but four died of injuries received because they missed the net. There is the unforgettable scene of the old lady hanging out of a window held from above by a *Vopo*, while below, young Westerners are pulling at her legs. Finally she dropped into safety and was whisked away to hospital.

On the back of the dustjacket of this book is the unforgettable photograph of the old lady about to drop. A little further down the street, workmen watched over by frontier guards were already bricking up the entrance to a church in the Bernauerstrasse which lay in the East but the doorway of which was exactly on the border. Now it has been demolished to make way for the death strip and the graffiti-covered concrete Wall. In the apartment block at No. 1 Bernauerstrasse there were only four inhabitants left and workmen were swarming through the flats, bricking up the windows and doors. It was 19 August and at lunchtime the workers left for a break. Two men in their late fifties, Rudolf Urban and his friend Willi Kutzminski, used this chance to tie a rope to a window on the first floor. First they lowered their wives to safety, and the two women managed to get down 4 metres with only a few grazes. In the meantime passers-by in the West had gathered and began to shout encouragement. Willi Kutzminski managed the descent without difficulty but tragedy struck when Urban was still on the rope. He heard heavy boots thundering up the staircase, panicked and let go. As the onlookers screamed, he fell 3 metres on to the pavement, landing with an ugly thud. Superficially he had only broken his ankle but on arrival in hospital it was discovered that he had severe internal injuries. The doctors fought in vain for four weeks to save the refugee's life, but he died as a result of the fall.

By 22 August, the teams of workmen had turned their attention to No. 48 where the 58-year-old widow Ina Siekman lived on the third floor – in the same flat in which she had been born. Acting probably on impulse, as she heard the police enter the building, she threw a few personal possessions out of the window, climbed out on to the sill and then jumped. She survived the impact for only a few seconds. Two hours later, just up the road, work was already in progress to replace the wire with concrete blocks. A young woman took a chance to climb over a remaining stretch of wire but was caught up by her clothes. Two guards saw her as she tried to free herself and shouted for her to stay still. Then she managed to break free and one of the guards fired a warning shot, while from the West, two policemen who happened to be at the spot, threw teargas grenades between the woman and her pursuers. The guards then opened fire and several shots hit buildings on the West side of the street. On all fours she managed to crawl to safety, unwounded but terrified.

On the front of the dustjacket of this book is a photograph taken on 15 August which went around the world. It became almost a symbol of the Berlin situation at the time, and the soldier in question was interviewed on television several times during the recent 25th anniversary. In addition, he was reunited in Berlin with the man who took that famous shot and the story was retold in countless magazine articles.

On the morning of 15 August, Conrad Schumann was on duty in the Bernauerstrasse. He unslung his machine pistol and pointed it at a group of six young men who were messing around in a suspicious manner with the barbed wire on the newly created demarcation line. He shouted at them to stop and they obeyed. He turned and called for reinforcements, and an officer ran up. 'What are you doing here? Get back from the frontier at once' he ordered them, while Schumann kept them covered. Then all six pulled out identity cards as members of the State Security Service. 'We just wanted to check that you are awake, comrades', they said. Conrad Schumann was puzzled. He remembered: 'it seemed to me stupid that the State Security had to stoop to such tricks to check on their own frontier troops.'

At the time this happened, the young sergeant had been on duty for forty-eight hours without a break, together with six soldiers from his platoon. Their job was to guard the corner of the Ruppinerstrasse against 'western militarists, white slavers and provokers' as it was expressed in their orders. Schumann was a volunteer who had signed on for seventeen years in the Peoples' Army, after having completed his basic training. Guarding the rolls of barbed wire was boring – ten paces one way and ten paces the other for two whole days. On either side his fellow soldiers marched up and down, like Schumann being constantly abused from the other side of the wire. Demonstrators called them swine, traitors, concentration camp guards, and it was not easy to remain unmoved and uninvolved while simply doing one's duty. From the corner of his eye, the sergeant observed the scene around him, which in fact moved him far more than the torrent of insults. He saw how a young woman in the East passed flowers over to her mother in the West. 'I heard the daughter wish her mother a happy birthday and say that she would not be able to come over and visit her any more. "Those here won't let me over".' 'Those here' were himself and his comrades. Looking back later he remembered: 'It was personal impressions like that that gave me far more food for thought than all the abuse.'

Schumann began to consider the impact of his activities. 'I thought about the fact that we lived in a so-called workers' and peasants' state. Our job was to protect socialism and our citizens. But then it dawned on me that the border defences were directed far more against our own people in the DDR than against the supposed class enemy.'

Such thoughts caused him to doubt more and more the justification of his duty although as a soldier he had to obey orders. It came into his head to ask why people should not be able to go where they wanted to. In political instruction he had been told about Western aggressors, bloodthirsty militarists and fascists who were the enemy, but where were they? He had not seen any, and on the contrary, the tanks were on his side of the wire. On the other side, all that he could see was the occasional policeman strolling by.

At midday the young sergeant was witness to another event that was to clarify his thoughts still further. Only a few hundred metres away from his post was the Arconaplatz and there a large demonstration began to gather, certainly more than a thousand people, something unheard of in the DDR. He heard vague chants and words like 'freedom' filtered through from the distance. But then this mass of people began to advance down the Ruppinerstrasse towards his section of the border. 'I thought that they would overrun us. I was nervous. I didn't know what to do. We had been told not to open fire and I wouldn't have done so anyway.' While such thoughts were running through Schumann's mind, armoured personnel carriers drove out of the side streets and soldiers advanced against the demonstrators with fixed bayonets, pushing them back. 'I will never forget how some of the people stood their ground with their arms crossed and cried out – "Go on, shoot, shoot, you cowards".'

Shortly afterwards he noticed that concrete breeze blocks and posts were being unloaded from lorries in a side street, and then a crane arrived. One of his comrades remarked that a wall was going to be built. Schumann realised that if he was going to make a run for it to the West, it would have to be soon. Otherwise they would all be walled in. At about 2 o'clock that afternoon he began to make his preparations. Carefully he watched his comrades who were on guard in his immediate vicinity, and when their backs were turned he began to press down with the tips of his fingers on the waist high wire strands. He reckoned that with a short run he would be able to jump over. But just at that moment one of the other soldiers turned round and asked him what he was up to. Schumann answered: 'the wire is starting to rust already'.

On the other side of the divide a considerable number of curious Westerners had assembled. There was a camera crew there and a press photographer, Klaus Lehnartz, who had been up and down the border since Sunday looking for good shots. He had always gravitated back to the Bernauerstrasse because of the frequent escapes there from the houses directly on the frontier. On the afternoon in question, he was sitting in his car when he noticed the young soldier fiddling about with the wire. Instinctively he felt that this was somehow odd. Parking his car he got out with his camera and walked into the middle of the street to watch. 'Every few minutes the soldier went back to the same piece of wire and pressed it down, a bit more at a time – while looking around carefully at his own people. My God, I thought, perhaps he is going to make a run for it.' Lehnartz made sure his camera was ready.

Schumann saw the man with the camera on the other side of wire. 'He didn't bother me at all. The more watchers there were on the Western side, the safer would be my flight. I knew from my experience that the presence of observers always made us more cautious.' He then carried on patrolling, but very close to the wire. 'Suddenly a young man from the West came up right close to me. I went towards him and shouted out loudly so that my comrades could hear, "get back immediately", but then whispered, "I am going to make a run for it".' The young man was somewhat startled but went off to the nearby police station and told the officers there that a People's Army soldier was going to escape. Four officers then climbed into a Volkswagen minibus which they parked discreetly in the Bernauerstrasse just as if they were carrying out a routine patrol. Just as discreetly they kept their eyes on the soldier.

Conrad Schumann by that time had managed to press down the barbed wire so that it was only knee-high. He took the magazine out of his weapon in case it should drop out when he jumped, or he should accidently catch the trigger. It was shortly before 4 o'clock and Schumann waited for the moment when the soldiers on either side of him would be at the far end of their respective beats. 'In the second before I made my run I felt my knees go weak. I was trembling.' He moved back about 10 metres and then sprinted for the wire, the nails in his boots hammering on the cobbles. Eyes turned towards him as Klaus Lehnartz looked through the viewfinder. A camera crew, realising that something was about to happen, began to film. Then he leaped, one hand flung out to steady himself and the other holding the sling of his weapon, which he dropped once he landed in the West. All he heard were the shouts of his comrades as he ran towards the police minibus, pulling off his steel helmet as he climbed inside. One of the policemen then ran towards the wire and picked up the discarded machine pistol.

Schumann was driven away to the main police station at Wedding where he was given a cigarette. As the press hovered around, coffee and sandwiches were provided. Headlines were telephoned through to the newspapers and Lehnartz did well with his photograph, which was a world scoop. Schumann himself was then handed over to the French authorities in whose sector he had landed, for interrogation, and then passed on to the Americans who kitted him out with new clothes. Today he lives in West Germany.

In an interview given after his escape, he made the following points.

It was drummed into us throughout our training and in particular during political instruction that our enemies were Western warmongers, militarists and revanchists. As I have since discovered, we had a completely false picture of the realities in the other part of Germany and in West Berlin. We were in no way prepared for the methods of securing the border as everything was highly secret. In those first few days we found that we were on our own and nobody bothered about us. There were only three orders. In our sector we were not to allow anyone to proceed from East to West, we should not react to provocation from the West and we should not open fire with live ammunition. . . . Nothing was organised. We had to find ourselves somewhere to sleep in the empty houses in the Bernauerstrasse. Now and again we were able to take turns for a few hours sleep on old blankets. There was nothing proper to eat. All we got was a plate of soup. That tended to depress both myself and my comrades.

In East Berlin, there was a mixture of desperation and resignation. Hundreds of would-be travellers to the West gathered around the Friedrichstrasse S-bahn station under the watching eyes of police and even a few tanks. The really enterprising ones had managed to slip away in the first two days, but even so the frontier was too long and the manpower was not available to do a really thorough sealing job. One favourite area was in the US sector to the south of the city centre, where an area of allotments fronted by a drainage ditch formed the border. On the Sunday a fence of posts and wire had been erected along the ditch, plus a few foxholes for the guards. In spite of this, quite a number of refugees managed to cross, encouraged by allotment holders who jeered at the soldiers. One group even made a raft to cross the ditch on which they loaded their precious mopeds. One of those helping others to escape was a young girl, Ursula Heinemann, who until the Sunday had crossed over daily to work as a waitress at a West Berlin hotel. At that stage she did not attempt to get away as she still believed that the sealing of the border was only temporary and that she would be able to return legally to her job. A week later, though, she realised that the Wall was to be permanent and that as a former worker in the West she could well be sent off to a collective farm far away from Berlin.

On the Saturday afternoon, Ursula, accompanied by her mother, went for a walk down the south-east of the city and ended up past the Teltow Canal where the allotment gardens were situated. Acting on impulse, she told her mother to wait, and opening a gate, slipped into the garden of a small weekend bungalow. There seemed to be nobody about and at the end of the garden Ursula found a barbed wire fence. Getting down flat on her stomach she lifted the lowest strand and managed to crawl underneath, only to find that between her and the drainage ditch a second fence had been put up. Again she succeeded in wriggling underneath although she could see a plume of cigarette smoke rising on the still afternoon air to her right. Nearly fainting with fear she scrambled through the ditch and was accosted on the far side by a man who con- gratulated her on escaping. Scratched and with her clothes torn by the wire, she accepted a cigarette from him. All she had with her was a handkerchief and her identity card, but a woman passer-by gave her two marks for the bus fare. Still dishevelled, she reported for work at the hotel.

On the evening of 23 August, Emil Goltz walked out of his flat, leaving his wife and daughter behind and without telling them what he intended to do. For several days he had argued with his wife but she had refused to make an escape attempt. Emil, however, had been casting around for a way out and had found one – by train. When the Underground and S-bahn had been severed, there was just one trans-border rail connection left. This was the S-bahn line running from Friedrichstrasse station in the East to Zoologischergarten in the West, a stretch of track which is also used by the few international trains that cross through the city. Emil had noticed that the Moscow– Paris express arrived at the Ostbahnhof at 10 o'clock in the evening and remained there for almost twenty minutes while three of the coaches were uncoupled. During this operation the train was unguarded in the station, and police arrived only a few minutes before departure to check the papers of those going on board. His plan was to sneak under the train and wedge himself on the brake connecting rods under one of the coaches for the short ride into the British sector.

That evening he took the S-bahn to the Ostbahnhof, but instead of joining the other passengers streaming towards the exit, he lingered on the platform. There was nobody about and across the intervening tracks he could see the express parked. Trying to look as though he had every right, he went to the end of the platform and made his way over the tracks, sheltered by the darkness, and came up at the rear of the express where he ducked down underneath the last coach. Heaving himself up on to the slippery grease-covered brake rods he hung on, the hard metal digging into his body. Below he could see the sleepers and he heard the crunch of boots as *Vopos* began to patrol along the tracks. Then slowly the train began to move off, through several stations where there was no stop. Emil clung on to the shaking vibrating rods, bruised all over, as they pulled in to Friedrichstrasse where there was a ten-minute halt, the last in the East. Again the *Vopos* patrolled, but none of them bothered to look underneath. After the agonising wait, there was a hiss of steam and the train was off on the long curve behind the Reichstag building and then through the Lehrter station the first in the West, without stopping. When the train halted a few moments later in the Zoo station, a cramped and bruised Emil Goltz lowered himself to the ground, liberally coated with grime, and reported to the police.

Those early escapes had been comparatively easy and were often spur-of-the-moment decisions over a frontier the defences of which had hardly been perfected. As the weeks went by, however, more and more ingenuity and courage were to be required. The one event that was to bring home to the world the sheer inhumanity of the DDR regime was the brutal killing of 17-year-old Peter Fechter, right under the eyes of crowds of spectators and a television camera team. The following morning the whole world was aware of what happened as they witnessed the slow death of a teenager. He was one of a Red Youth labour squad who had all decided to escape but one by one the rest had dropped out, leaving Peter and one companion to make the attempt. It is probable that one of the original group had betrayed the escape attempt, for Peter and his friend were under observation the moment they approached the border. They had chosen a point some 200 metres to the right of Checkpoint Charlie where a large building (since demolished) was right behind the Wall on the Eastern side. The Wall itself at that point was made of breeze blocks about 2 metres high and topped with barbed wire.

Just before 2 o'clock in the afternoon, the two youths hid themselves in the disued building and then made a dash for the Wall. Peter's friend managed to pull himself up and through the wire to drop safely in the West under a hail of bullets. Peter Fechter was caught as he tried to get through the wire and then fell back to the base of the wall, hit by several shots. The sound of firing brought a crowd of spectators to the scene in the West, many of whom climbed on to car roofs to get a view of what was happening. On the other side, *Vopos* formed a ring around the body but made no attempt to help the dying boy, who every now and again cried out for help in a voice getting weaker and weaker as the time passed. Overhead a helicopter hovered and tension mounted as the crowd in the West began to chant and jeer, accusing the *Vopos* of being murderers. Police threw a first aid kit over the Wall but it hit the wire and burst open. It was nearly an hour before the guards in the East made a move. They threw teargas grenades to try to hide the body with a smokescreen and chucked others over the wall to try to disperse the angry crowd. As the camera shutters clicked, West Berlin police replied by throwing teargas at their counterparts in the East, who by then were kneeling over the injured boy, although without making any effort to help him.

Peter Fechter bled slowly to death, taking about an hour finally to die. Like a limp rag doll the body was finally picked up by two guards who carried it away from the wall and dumped it unceremoniously in the back of a van, which then drove off. The crowds lingered on until nightfall, talking quietly among themselves. For several days afterwards there were mass demonstrations in the city and Russian troops and diplomats were stoned and abused. Routine protests were exchanged between the Russians and Americans, and the latter were blamed by the Berliners for having failed to take action. The local people simply could not understand why the Western Allies did not send in tanks and just batter down the Wall. Anti-American feeling became endemic among West Berliners for many years, and even the charismatic visit of Kennedy did little to dispel it.

Only a few days after the death of Fechter, there was another border 'incident' with a fatal conclusion. The following is the text of a police statement that, greatly enlarged, was put up against the Wall facing East as a form of 'wanted' poster.

On 29 August at 14.10 hours, an unknown man made an

attempt as a refugee to evade the officials of the soviet Zone of Occupation, by swimming the Teltow Canal in the vicinity of the Wupperstrasse located in Berlin Lichterfelde. The frontier between the territory of Berlin and that of the Zone runs through the middle of the canal. According to witnesses, this refugee had already reached the frontier by swimming, when he was hit mortally by at least one shot emanating from a firearm in the hands of a frontier guard of the Soviet Zone Occupation. Among those who were firing from the Soviet Zone bank of the Teltow Canal was the man whose picture appears alongside. A reward of 10,000 DM (West) is hereby offered for factual information that could lead to the discovery of persons who have made themselves liable to prosecution in connection with the death of the refugee.

This sober official statement is followed by the confidential telephone numbers of the Berlin murder squad. As far as both Berlin and West German authorities were concerned, a frontier guard from the DDR who shot at and killed a refugee was guilty of murder and, as a German citizen, could be tried and sentenced by them. This naturally brings out the age-old question which surfaced again and again as a defence in war crimes trials, the plea of 'I was only obeying orders'. Naturally, if one assumes that the DDR was and is a sovereign state and entitled to give its troops direct orders to shoot to kill, then such a defence must stand. The West Germans, however, did not recognise the DDR and claimed to be acting for all of Germany. At the Teltow Canal, a young border guard, Fritz Hanke, was stationed in January 1963. While on duty he shot at and killed a certain Max Samland who was trying to swim through the icy water. It was only several weeks later that the bullet-riddled body was recovered. In the meanwhile, however, Hanke had escaped himself, and as a guard, was naturally subjected to thorough interrogation by the security authorities. From this it transpired that he had been on duty that fateful night and he was put on trial for participation in a murder. Hanke was duly sentenced to fifteen months in prison, a light punishment but given as a warning to other guards that they could not escape moral responsibility for their actions.

The authorities in the East used this to stiffen the resolve of the border guards by warning them that if they escaped, they would be imprisoned in the West. In spite of this, however, within two years of the Wall being built, 2200 frontier troops fled over the Berlin or West German frontiers.

The text of the actual order is:

> If suspicious persons are in the vicinity of the border, order them to stop. If they proceed further in the direction of the demarcation line, fire two warning shots in the air. If this step fails, shoot low to wound. If this fails, shoot to kill.

It is not easy to look inside the minds of the guards one can glimpse while looking over the Wall from an observation stand in West Berlin. Most are young conscripts and are liable to severe punishment if they are caught even smiling at people in the West. In some cases it would seem that guards have been too ready to shoot to kill, but from interrogation of those who have escaped it is clear that their one great fear is having to make use of firearms. Although they are trained to regard the west as 'enemy territory' they live and work in an officially fostered atmosphere of distrust. The one-time sergeant-major Hans-Jurgen Hentze, who escaped in January 1981, made the following comment:

> When the Company's duty starts there is always a feeling of tension. They mostly hope that no refugees will come, or as I have heard from several members of my unit, that hopefully they will not have to open fire. That was what I feared most. One notices it mostly when there is a search on. Then you often hear the lads saying, 'I hope that he doesn't come into my sector'. One can hardly describe the tension and nervousness among the border guards in such a situation.

To end this chapter it is worth considering extracts from a lengthy statement issued after his escape by the *Grepo*, Dieter Jentzen. He leapt to freedom from a height of 8 metres, thereby suffering from such severe foot injuries that he had to spend nearly two years in hospital.

I should like to say a few words on behalf of my excomrades. All too often people tend to see the potential murderer in the 'guardians of the Wall'. I am convinced that the number of those captured at the Wall and of those shot would be at least ten times as high if those serving there were merely blindly carrying out orders. The privates and NCO's at the Wall, who are not there because they want to be but because they were drafted there, should be seen as people who do not wish to gain an advantage for themselves at the cost of the fugitives.

The guard who makes suggestions for improving the border security system and reports anything that looks suspicious, and has a good service record – for example, many arrests – will gain rapid promotion, extra leave, pay and other privileges. And yet most of them forego such advantages. Whoever can endure never speaking to another person in confidence does not have to fear being denounced. . . . Most of the soldiers ask themselves, what would I do if confronted by an escapee? Or better, what can I do to avoid being confronted with an escapee? Therefore I appeal to everyone in West Berlin or West Germany who visits the border, to see through the uniform. Occasionally, as members of the Peoples' Army, we were stared at like animals in a cage. Many times I have heard abuse and the next minute been shouted at to come over. But it is extremely important to show the man in uniform at the border that his difficult situation is understood and that we are thankful to him for not gaining easily acquired advantages at the expense of others. What we occasionally heard on the Western radio and what we occasionally read on the border placards proved to be the exact opposite to the troops. On the anniversary of August 13, one border placard read – Don't shoot, think! That is precisely the sort of language that should be avoided. For the soldier must assume that the people in the 'Golden West' consider themselves more intelligent and look up to these soldiers. It may be thought to be of no importance for future political developments what we say to the 50,000 men on the border through Germany, who can be reached so easily, and what attitude we take towards them. Such a view proves that we have been incapable of seeing beyond those in power and of establishing an alliance from person to person. For this alliance – which could be effective not merely between fellow countrymen but also between Europeans and the Russian people – this alliance is precisely what Ulbricht fears more than tanks.

The above was written by a young man in his twenties, in the days when Walther Ulbricht still ruled the DDR on Stalinist principles. The sad thing is that little has changed and his successors still order their minions to shoot at people attempting to cross a border – in spite of the Helsinki Agreement.

4
Individual Courage

The very existence of the Wall and the resulting social dis-
location caused a variety of people from all sorts of walks of
life to find within themselves reserves of courage – which under
normal circumstances might never have been called for. This
chapter deals with a number of escapes that were planned and
carried out by individuals without the help of outsiders. In
September 1961, shortly after the Wall had appeared, 29
youngsters entered the Max Planck High School in East Berlin
to start their five-year course as the future elite of the nation.
The authorities of the DDR saw in such carefully selected
teenagers a fruitful field for political and patriotic indoctrination, but by putting all the clever ones together managed
only to stimulate the freedom of thought. Many of that particular class, which represented a good cross-section of any
East German high school, were far more fascinated by the
concept of freedom, the chance to study without propaganda
and even the simple lure of Western consumerism. By 1964,
as they grew into young adults, the theme of escape was a
common subject of conversation and was to lead to a whole
series of reprisals, especially as the deputy headmaster was an
agent of the State Security apparatus. But what was initially
merely idle speculation crystallised when the first of their
classmates escaped.

Three of the students had managed to obtain some Western
cigarettes and were accused of having begged them from tourists, and one of them, Jurgen Klembt, was expelled from the

49

school. He then disappeared and his friends discovered that he had made a successful escape, equipped with West German papers. Immediately after 13 August it had been fairly simple to get hold of a forged West German identity card or a foreign passport. Students at various art schools developed a thriving cottage industry in forgery, but then the authorities put a stop to that by introducing secret marks on to the papers of all those entering East Berlin. After a number of arrests and mutual accusations of betrayal, the escape helpers discovered the system of such marks and were once again able to fool the guards, but not for long. The next step was the introduction of foreign exchange certificates for all visitors. These had to be filled in at the frontier stating how much money the visitor had with him and how much he had exchanged at the official rate. A duplicate was kept at the border post and compared with the original when the visitor left. Without the certificate that matched up with a duplicate, there was no chance of forging suitable exit papers. What had actually happened in the case of Jurgen Klembt only came to light when a 17-year-old West German appeared in court in East Berlin, accused of having given his papers to the lad. In his defence he stated that the papers had been stolen from his coat when he was at a dance hall, but even so, he was awarded eight months in prison.

The classmates began to concentrate on finding a way out for themselves in spite of their awareness of the risks involved. From Western radio broadcasts they discovered that 30 per cent of inmates in East German prisons had been sentenced for 'attempting to flee the republic' and that by the beginning of 1964, 5000 years of prison had been awarded by the courts to escapees who had been caught. Three lads in particular, Klaus Herrmann, Holger Klein and Peter Riese, decided to escape together and used every weekend to try to find a way over the wall. It was Klaus Herrmann who believed that he had the answer and one day took the other two to the Luisen Cemetery, the same spot where Wolfgang Fuchs was later to pull off one of his best planned coups (see Chapter 5). The cemetery ends at the Wall, on the other side of which and in the West is the Liesenstrasse. The three youngsters managed to talk their way into the cemetery armed with a watering can

7. *The Brandenburg Gate – walled in.*

8. *A watchtower guards the Teltow Canal.*

9. *The death of Peter Fechter.*

10. *Peter Fechter's body is carried away.*

11. *Tunnel digging.*

12. *At work in Tunnel 57.*

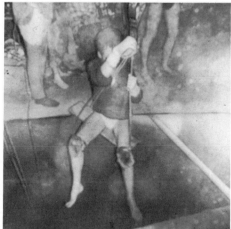

14. *A child is hauled out of a tunnel.*

13. *A refugee crawls through Tunnel 57 to freedom.*

16. An East German guard escapes.

15. Made it!

17. An East German guard shuns the camera.

and at first stood piously in front of a grave. They were, however, discovered by a frontier guard when they tried to move nearer to the wall. He let them go but as in so many cases in Berlin, they were discovered because they were betrayed. Obviously they had discussed what happened with other pupils and when, three months later, a girl at the school was picked up by the police for a totally different offence, she was promised her freedom in return for the names of anyone she knew who was planning to escape. The three boys were pulled in for questioning at school and then interrogated by the police. As nothing could really be proved against them, they were released but then expelled from school, which in practice meant that any worthwhile career in the DDR was barred to them in the future.

The next to be expelled was Wolfgang Schulze. His natural father had spent six years in prison for political offences in the Soviet Zone after the war and on his release had moved to West Berlin where he had remarried. Wolfgang's mother had also remarried, to a senior official in the Communist Party, and Wolfgang himself was a functionary in the FDJ – the Communist Youth Movement. In the summer of 1964, Wolfgang visited his grandmother who lived in the Harz Mountains near the frontier to West Germany. While there he made a reconnaissance of the border but was caught 500 metres from the fence. His excuse was that he had lost his way while out for a stroll but the result was inevitable – expulsion. A few weeks later he was in West Berlin, and on arrival took a taxi to his father's address – to a man whom he could not remember.

Wolfgang had discovered the escape method himself and had made the attempt alone after his close friend decided to back out, but he gave the necessary information to one or two other trusted friends. Four more from the same school came out that way plus two from another high school in East Berlin. In the previous chapter, mention was made of an escape using the trans-zonal trains whose last stop in East Berlin is at the Friedrichstrasse station. From there they pass into the West over a curving viaduct, moving comparatively slowly. The scheme was to climb up on to the viaduct just outside the station and to leap on to the running board of a train which would be moving at a speed of about 20 kilometres per hour.

The chosen train was the Warsaw–Aachen express which departed from Friedrichstrasse at 20.53 hours every evening. The next group to make the attempt consisted of Klaus Herrmann, Holger Klein, a lad known as 'Kalle' and Frank Thomascheit. Only the latter knew the method. Shortly after 8 o'clock they met near the station where Frank told them that only two at a time could go – the other two would have to wait for the Moscow–Paris express which left at 22.27 hours. He then led them a short distance along the bank of the River Spree and down a side street beside the viaduct until they came to a passage under the bridge that gave access to a coal yard. When they got there, however, they found a man loitering around, his coat collar turned up to hide his face. At first they assumed that they had been betrayed, but he made no move to arrest them. So Klaus and Holger kept an eye on the stranger and tried to distract him, while Frank and 'Kalle' climbed up the viaduct at a point where several stones had been broken out of the wall. From there they had to swing themselves up into the metal girders which supported the track, cross over to the other side and hide in a niche. On top, however, 'Kalle' lost his nerve and jumped off, a height of 5 metres. Looking down, Frank saw him lying on the ground and the man with the turned-up coat collar was standing over him. But then he heard in the distance the station loudspeaker announcing the departure of the train. Frank heard the release of steam and then the track was covered by smoke and he scrambled out of the niche and over the guard rails alongside the track. Then he ran and managed to grab the handrail at the door of one of the last coaches. At first he could only kneel on the running board but then with an extra heave he managed to stand upright and open the door. Blackened with soot and grease, he slipped into the toilet and bolted the door. Minutes later the train thundered over a bridge which was the actual sector border and pulled into the Zoo station in West Berlin. There on the platform were four of his classmates to welcome him, but Frank could only tell them that he would be the last one. The secret was known to the authorities.

'Kalle's' fall had not been observed by Klaus and Holger

who after following the man with the turned-up collar for a while, had lost him. They returned to the spot an hour later and climbed up as the coast seemed to be clear. Once on top they became separated, and then Klaus heard on the loud-speaker that the train would be delayed for twenty minutes. He decided to have a look for the niche, but while crossing the track was challenged by a voice coming from the darkness: 'Hey you. What are you doing on railway property?' Not knowing whether the shout was for him or Holger, he quickly let himself down to the ground and slipped away – assuming that his companion had been caught. In the meantime, Frank and the reception committee had gone off for a beer, having decided not to wait for the later train as they assumed that the discovery of 'Kalle' would mean that the escape route was blown. Holger, however, made it out that night and turned up the following morning at the flat where Wolfgang Schultze had moved in with his father. Their problem was that they could not warn Klaus not to make another attempt by the same route, which they were agreed was by then bound to have been sealed off.

In the meantime Klaus visited the site in daylight, and saw to his surprise that nothing seemed to have altered. There were a few passers-by and no obvious plain clothes police, extra wire or uniformed guards. So that night at 20.30 he went back to the station and down beside the viaduct. Thirteen minutes before the train was due to leave he climbed the wall, but as he did so a passing couple stopped and stared at him. They did not say anything but walked swiftly away with ample time to warn the police at the station. Klaus was in a quandary, but decided to carry on regardless of the risk, and at first hid himself among the girders in the darkness. He considered that he had nothing to lose. Both his parents were already in West Berlin and, by then, some of his best friends. He heard the distorted sound of the station announcement that the train was about to leave, and risked a peep on to the track. Above him he had heard the crunching of heavy boots, and he saw two sentries wandering slowly along the track, looking around and, from time to time, over the railings. But then the train began to move on to the viaduct and as the locomotive passed him it belched out a dense cloud of smoke. Using this as cover, Klaus swung himself over the railings and sprinted alongside the swaying coaches. There were twelve in all and he missed the first two because of the smoke. Then, when he could see again the next coaches did not have handrails, only door handles. Running along the stone track bed almost out of breath his hopes began to fade, but the last but one coach had a handrail reaching right down to the running board. Klaus managed to grab it and with a heave he was up and in through the door.

Minutes later, he too arrived at the Zoo station where Holger and Wolfgang were waiting on the platform, not expecting to meet him, but with the intention of asking other passengers if they had seen anyone being led away under arrest. None of them could understand why after the discovery of the injured 'Kalle' there had not been a massive security operation at the escape spot. They soon found out that Kalle had been arrested and that the place where they had climbed up had been secured with alarm signal wires. Surely the mysterious man with the up-turned collar had been a State Security agent. Thus it was with great surprise that a couple of weeks later, fitted out with new clothes, three of the pupils met the man again. Frank, Holger and Klaus went to a government building to deal with some paperwork when they saw him in the corridor. Getting into conversation, the man complained: 'you lot made it damned difficult for me. Every time I wanted to climb up on the bridge, one of your lot turned up.' He went on to tell them that when 'Kalle' had fallen down, he had helped him up and that the lad was arrested after rumours about his injuries had circulated around the school.

The pupils gave a press conference which was carried by West Berlin television, and was naturally seen by their fellow pupils in the East. This prompted one of the girls in the class to make an attempt, and a couple of months later she arrived having crawled under barbed wire and through a ditch to freedom. Thus nearly half a classroom of 17-year-olds managed to get away and build up new lives in the West where they could study without political indoctrination and without the ever present fear of denunciation and prison.

So far we have been looking at how Germans worked out

the solution to a German problem, but one Englishman also became involved with the Wall. In the summer of 1965, Phillip Hewitt, who was in between school and university, went to Dresden in East Germany as a member of a youth working party. They were helping to rebuild a hospital which had been destroyed during the British air raids in 1945. While there he met a young girl called Ilse Schulz who came from East Berlin, and the two fell in love. Phillip went back to England and to university, but as he was studying German anyway, he paid a number of visits to Ilse in East Berlin. A year later they became engaged and started to take the necessary steps to get married, but soon found themselves in a bureaucratic tangle with the authorities. Getting desperate, Phillip decided to take the law into his own hands, and began to cast around for ways and means of getting Ilse over to the West. He soon realised that the Wall was far too difficult a nut to crack and that the answer was to try to exit through another Eastern bloc state where the controls were not so strict. Basically, Phillip planned to use a British passport showing the two of them as a married couple.

The first problem was to get hold of a suitable document and then to make a convincing forgery. He took his parents' passport and levered off their photographs, substituting pictures of himself and Ilse. He forged the Foreign Office embossed stamp by running over the outline from the back with a pointed object, and crudely altered the handwritten personal descriptions page. Equipped with this, he went to the Czech Consulate in London and they stamped in a transit visa for Mr and Mrs Hewitt. This was necessary, as the possession of a legitimate visa would help to establish the genuineness of the passport. The next stage was for Phillip to travel on his own passport to West Berlin and cross into the East on the forged one, a ploy which worked, except for the fact that the authorities on the border wrote in ink under the East German visa – 'Mr Hewitt is travelling alone'. That meant that the two of them could not leave the DDR as an English married couple – Ilse would have to travel to the Czech border on her own passport and in no-man's-land they would have to switch papers, hoping that the Czech guards would not be able to read German.

Phillip felt committed by then. It was shortly before Christmas 1966 that they boarded a crowded train for the three-hour journey to the border via Dresden. Ilse sat in a compartment with five Czechs and Phillip got a seat in the next one. Feeling that they might never see each other again, he then took her for a meal in the restaurant car, but neither of them could eat with any enthusiasm. What follows is Phillip's description of events:

> I could feel my stomach screwing itself up into a ball, as I thought of the moment when I would have to do the switch to show one set of documents to one set of border guards and the other set to the next. Ilse was leaving East Germany with her own passport and had no connection with me, and yet within a minute, or half a minute, or twenty seconds – I didn't know how long – I would have to produce the husband/wife papers and say this is my wife next door. I didn't know how the people in the compartment would react to seeing her produce a light-blue identity card one minute and then maybe only seconds later to seeing this bearded gentleman at the door with a British passport.

It was at that most difficult stage of the operation that the plan nearly came unstuck.

> It was tricky because I didn't know how much time there would be between the two different passport examinations. In fact we only had about 35 seconds to do the switch. I'd just shown my papers to the East German border guards and they'd left the compartment. I gave them ten seconds to get down the corridor a bit, but when I emerged, lo and behold the Czechs were coming from the opposite direction which I hadn't counted on at all. So there I was, standing in the corridor with a passport and two Czech visa forms, with my 'wife' in a compartment full of Czechs all going home for Christmas. I gave the papers to the guards and said this is my wife and this is me, and nobody said a word. In the corner was a pale-faced Ilse and five unknown and rather astonished Czech faces looking at me. I've respected them ever since for that gesture of solidarity. Any one of them

could have said to the guard in Czech, which I could not understand anyway, there's something wrong here. This is an East German and we have never seen that man before.

Feeling very relieved, the Hewitts arrived legitimately in Prague where they had to find a hotel for the night. The following day they left on the express for Vienna, travelling first class as those were the only seats they could get, but the border crossing into Austria was an anticlimax. The forged passport excited no interest, but even so, they went to the dining car and bought a bottle of champagne. After a few days in Vienna to recuperate, they left for England, where Phillip had to confess and face the music. The Passport Office authorities were not amused but in the circumstances decided against prosecution although they did confiscate the forgery. The Hewitts later returned to West Germany, where Phillip now runs a language school and translation agency.

Another young couple whose love was to be dogged with similar problems were Margit Tharau and Hans-Peter Meixner. They met by chance at a wedding in East Berlin, where she lived with her mother, while he, an Austrian, was studying in West Berlin. Soon they started seeing each other regularly, as he could legitimately cross into the DDR and had no intention of organising an escape. When they became engaged they imagined that it would be simple to apply for the necessary documents and to arrange a wedding, after which Margit would be permitted to leave as the wife of a foreigner. As in the case of the Hewitts, months went by, traipsing from office to office, filling out forms and waiting. When one application was refused, they submitted another one, as hope slowly began to fade. It was at this stage that Hans-Peter began to toy with the idea of an escape. On his regular trips into the East in his Opel, he noticed how carefully the car was checked for hidden compartments and realised that there was no chance of bringing anyone through in the boot. Now at that time, in the mid 1960s, Checkpoint Charlie was still a fairly simple affair, little more than a large compound with a lifting pole at each end. The flash of inspiration came by accident as one evening, after a visit to Margit, Hans-Peter waited in a queue of cars to drive through to the West. Just in front of him was a small German sports car which started to roll forward and ended up with its bonnet wedged under the barrier. Up rushed the guards, guns at the ready, but the explanation was a simple one – the driver had forgotten to apply the handbrake.

On his next visit, Hans-Peter equipped himself with a tape measure, and as he drove slowly through the barrier, he judged its height in relation to the side of his car. Once inside the compound and while waiting for his papers to be examined, he got out and surreptitiously made a mark with his finger in the dirt on the bodywork, at the same height. As soon as he was clear of the border post he stopped and measured the distance between the mark and the ground, which was a fraction over 3 feet. If he was going to drive under the barrier, that was the maximum vehicle height to avoid getting wedged. Then the search began for a car for the dash to freedom. After several days of fruitless visits to secondhand dealers and scanning advertisements in the papers, Hans-Peter found what he was looking for at the premises of a car hire firm. This was an Austin-Healey Sprite with a detachable windscreen, which he hired for a week and drove through to the East the same evening. He explained to Margit that there was enough room to hide her behind the seats, but there remained the problem of her mother. Once her daughter had left she would be on her own in East Berlin, so it was decided that she should escape as well, crammed into the minute boot. At least then she would be able to live near the young couple, and was prepared to risk her life.

On a bombsite in West Berlin, Hans-Peter got down to some serious practice by simulating the conditions at the checkpoint, using old poles, bricks and dustbins. The actual compound was about a 100 metres long and at the end were three reinforced concrete walls, just wide enough apart to permit a vehicle to pass through them in a zig-zag path. This was designed to hinder any attempts to ram the barrier which was the last defence before the actual border into the American zone. Speed was of the essence and the young Austrian worked at it daily, building up his confidence with the car and learning to control it with a margin of safety. One evening in May 1963 he drove to Margit's flat for the last time, planning to return in the early hours on the following morning with the two ladies on board. He had to choose a time when there would be little traffic about at the checkpoint, so as to have a clear run and be able to build up speed. The only worry was if a car was coming in the opposite direction, but that was simply a risk that had to be accepted.

The women stuffed a few valuables and papers into their pockets and squeezed themselves into their hiding places. The boot lid was jammed down on top of the mother and Margit behind the seats was covered with a rug. Hans-Peter drove off through the dark streets and after a few minutes came to the barrier at the entrance where his passport was given only a cursory examination. Then the barrier was raised and he drove slowly into the compound trying not to look suspicious. Ahead he could see another guard waving him forward to the bay where cars were searched and when only a few metres away he jammed his foot hard down on the throttle and swung to the left, aiming for the gap in the first wall. Concrete flashed past as he steered to the right with tyres screaming and then lined up for the last gap. Through that there was only the pole. A last glance, then he had to duck his head down and drive blind, by then at nearly 30 miles an hour. The pole flashed overhead and they were through, without a shot having been fired, so surprised were the guards.

A few months afterwards a wedding was celebrated in West Berlin with the mother of the bride able to be present. Naturally enough the story of the escape received considerable publicity in the Western press, which was read by an Argentinian living in West Berlin and who was in a similar predicament – his girlfriend was in the Eastern part of the city. Believe it or not, he hired the same car and a week later pulled the same stunt. On his way out one of the guards said casually to him: 'Wasn't this the same car as we had through here the other day?'

But if you think that an Austin-Healey Sprite would be the smallest possible vehicle in which to smuggle out a person, you would be wrong. In the museum at Checkpoint Charlie, an Isetta bubble car is preserved for posterity, one of those odd-shaped conveyances that were developed at the end of the 1950s in Germany. It is a two-seater with a front opening door and a motorcycle engine in the back. An enterprising escape organiser noticed that the Isetta was never thoroughly checked by the East German border guards as it seemed impossible to hide anyone inside. But he found that by removing the heater and the air filter and substituting the petrol tank with a small 4-litre canister, just enough for a border crossing, a small person could be concealed on top of the engine and rear wheel. This amazing contraption is said to have made nine runs and one of them was filmed, showing how the hatch was opened and the refugee literally pulled out feet first. The rear suspension had to be stiffened so as to compensate for the weight of the refugees.

To continue on the theme of love recognising no frontiers, an eternal one in the context of the Berlin Wall, there is the astonishing tale of Hans Christian Cars. In April 1965 this young Swede, who was studying in Geneva, got on to a train in East Berlin bound for a short visit to Prague. He had not bothered to reserve a seat and the train, as is usual in Eastern Europe, was packed. Hans found himself jammed in the swaying corridor and was resigned to an uncomfortable journey, when he noticed a girl beckoning him into a compartment where there was a spare seat. She was an East Berliner, Isolade Giese, and was travelling to visit friends in Budapest. Originally she had reserved two seats, one for herself and one for another girl, who at the last moment had been unable to accompany her. The two young people chatted happily as far as Prague where Hans got off, with Isolade's address in Budapest on a piece of paper in his pocket. It had not been love at first sight, but Hans decided to spend a few days in Budapest as an excuse to see the girl once again. After that he visited her frequently at home in East Berlin, and as their love for each other grew, so did the realisation that there was no future unless Isolade could be brought out to the West. At each visit they discussed scheme after scheme only to dismiss each in turn – false compartments, stealing a boat on the Baltic, forged passports. Hans was obsessed by the idea that a successful escape had to be something original – something that had not been tried before, and by a process of elimination he came up with a daring scheme. He decided to fly Isolade out in a light aircraft.

That was fine, but the trouble was that he could not fly an aeroplane and as a student, had not enough money for the necessary instruction. By then back in Sweden, he managed to get a part-time job and started on a course of lessons in a Cessna in the autumn of 1965. Constantly bedevilled by bad weather and lack of funds, it was not until the following August that he received his licence, although he had been able to put in a good number of hours practising low flying and short take-offs. Equipped at last with the licence, Hans travelled down to Austria and hired a car in which he drove up and down the border area with Czechoslovakia, looking for a suitable meadow on the far side. When he had found what he was looking for, he crossed over the frontier and carefully examined the actual terrain, which he decided was possible for the operation. The next step was to hire a Cessna, fly it from Salzburg to an airfield near Vienna, and send a telegram to Isolade. This gave a rendezvous for a meeting at Brno in Czechoslovakia, to which she could travel without undue formalities. The couple met for a somewhat tense meal and then Hans drove her to the selected meadow where she was to hide in some bushes through the night. Hans explained that he would collect her the following morning, 20 August 1966, and then left her to drive back into Austria. Shortly after 7 o'clock he was sitting in the aircraft waiting for clearance to take off when ugly weather developed and a vicious storm broke out. That put paid to the flight, and the thoughts of Hans inevitably turned to Isolade, sitting soaked in the bushes. Cold, tired and hungry she realised that something had gone wrong, and made her way to the road where she hitched a lift into Bratislava where they had a back-up rendezvous in a small hotel. But unknown to her, when the weather cleared, Hans had decided to make an attempt and had actually flown into the meadow without any difficulty. Not seeing her there, he had taken off, again without any intervention from the watchtowers, no shots fired, no shouting guards on the ground below. Hans believed that if he had been seen, the border guards must have thought that he had strayed across the border by accident.

Once back at the airfield he collected his car and drove through to Bratislava where he met a worried Isolade. He had decided that a further flight into the same meadow was inviting trouble, so he loaded his fiancée into the car and they went off to find another suitable spot for a quick landing. After some time a field was located and Hans spent quite a while imprinting the landmarks in his mind, including a suitable church tower right in line with the landing direction. Leaving Isolade once again in hiding, he returned to Vienna to wait for morning.

The next day the weather was quite clear and he made a smooth take-off, heading East towards the frontier. Shortly after 8 o'clock, Isolade heard the noise of the approaching aircraft and saw it swoop down low over the border strip and come in to land. Hans turned at the far end of the field into the wind as Isolade ran towards him from her hiding place. The door opened, and she scrambled in as the engine was gunned to maximum revs. Bumping over the grass they were airborne in seconds and zoomed over the silent watchtowers into Austria and safety. The only jarring note was that when Isolade reported to the refugee camp, nobody would believe her story and for several weeks she was accused of being a spy.

Wolfgang Eulitz is a talented musician. Born in West Berlin, he had studied at the conservatory in the Soviet sector in the days before the Wall was built, living there as a boarder, where he met and fell for the 15-year-old Inge Lange. In the summer of 1961 he went off to Ireland to play the double bass in the Irish Radio Symphony Orchestra on a twelve-month engagement. For Wolfgang this was a good opportunity to gain experience and learn English, and both of them assumed that when his contract ended he would return and they would get married. But after he had been only a few weeks in Dublin the Wall was built, and in his letters Wolfgang promised that he would settle with Inge in East Berlin – she had had no intention of escaping at the time. Now, while in Dublin, he had registered with the West German Embassy and this factor enabled him to apply for a West German passport when his period in Ireland finished; in addition, when he returned he brought his Skoda car with Irish number plates. Once back in Berlin he visited Inge almost daily. She had found a flat for them and he began to ship over his possessions in the car. Everyone assumed that he was going to live over there but in fact he had started to consider ways and means of getting his fiancée to the West. This was the summer of 1962. The Wall was a year old but the defences were to a certain extent still in their infancy and vehicle searches were not so rigorous in those days. Wolfgang noticed that the guards did not look underneath cars; only in the boot and under the bonnet.

His plan was to strap Inge underneath, and he practised with his brother in West Berlin for several days, before informing Inge, who was not keen to go along with the plan. Wolfgang, however, was determined, and choosing a filthy wet night in October, when he knew the guards would be less than enthusiastic, he drove Inge to a bombsite. There he strapped her up tight against the chassis, wearing asbestos gloves to cling on to the exhaust pipe, her face only inches from the hot metal and her body only inches from the road. Just as he was finishing the job he was startled by a voice from behind – the voice of a policeman asking him if he needed any help. Trying to look calm, Wolfgang replied that he had had some trouble with the car but had managed to fix it, while Inge had a worm's eye view of a large pair of menacing boots.

Heading off towards the checkpoint at Heinrich Heine-strasse, he had to drive as slowly as possible to stop the suspension from bouncing, stopping every now and again to see if the girl underneath was still all right and in position. Once into the checkpoint, there was an agonising delay. Wolfgang had to go inside the control building where his papers were examined for a solid half an hour. Through the rain-soaked windows he could see guards wandering around, looking at the car with the Irish plates from time to time. Once outside, he still had to undergo the routine search in the compound. The guard was in no hurry and even wanted a chat as he poked around in the boot and behind the seats. Underneath, Inge was soaked to the skin and her hair had become unpinned and was trailing on the ground. Again, all she could see was concrete roadway and official boots. But finally the guard was satisfied and with his valuable freight still in place, Wolfgang drove through into West Berlin. Stopping a few hundred metres

63

inside the border, he hastened to unstrap Inge and lift her stiffened body into the car.

The foregoing are only a few examples of individually planned and executed escapes which received some publicity. Many others who succeeded simply faded quietly into Western society and have never spoken about their adventures, perhaps in the hope that their method would not be discovered and could possibly be used again. Others still keep quiet for fear of reprisals being taken against their relatives remaining in the East. This chapter ends, however, with a short account of the action of a very brave man on 13 September 1964. Private Hans Puhl was serving in Berlin as a military policeman in the United States Army, and although an American citizen, had emigrated from Germany only four years before. By chance he became mixed up in an escape attempt at the Wall, not far away from where Peter Fechter had been shot. Just after dawn, a young East German, Michael Meyer, made his bid for freedom at a point where he had to cross two barbed wire fences and the Wall itself. He was struggling over the first fence in the death strip when the guards opened fire. Getting down safely he ran for the second fence and, miraculously unhurt by a further fusillade, reached the bottom of the Wall. Two guards ran up and trained their guns on the young man as he crouched there, but when they became aware of a pair of West German policemen watching them from a nearby building they retreated, leaving their victim. At this stage, hearing the shots, Private Puhl had climbed up the stairs of a block of flats and was looking out of the window on the second floor.

As the guards retreated, the refugee made another effort, but was shot at and wounded five times The West Berlin police attempted to give covering fire, but the guards made another rush to the Wall to grab their helpless victim. Then Puhl intervened from his vantage point. Yelling at the guards to drop Michael Meyer he took aim with his rifle and threw a teargas grenade, after which he ran back down the stairs. Two civilians hoisted him up to the top on the Wall where he found himself staring into the muzzle of a pistol held by one of the guards – who once again had dropped the refugee. Puhl called out to him to lie still while they cut the wire on top of the Wall.

This was done by the two civilians, while the guards on the other side retreated into a trench from which they started firing at the American soldier clinging to the concrete blocks. He lowered a rope down to Meyer, who was by then too weak to grasp it properly. The problem was solved by some firemen who had arrived. They made a loop in the rope and shouted at the young man to pass this under his arms. Puhl and an American sergeant then pulled his bleeding body as gently as they could up the face of the Wall and heaved him over. On arrival, it was discovered that Meyer had been wounded in both thighs, an ankle, a hand and an arm, but none of the injuries were serious. For his courage, Puhl was presented with a certificate by the then Governing Lord Mayor of Berlin, Willi Brandt.

Another hero was Klaus Bruske, who although mortally wounded managed to crash a lorry packed with refugees through one of the checkpoints. He died minutes after arriving in the West.

5

Wolfgang Fuchs

Today, in his early forties, Wolfgang Fuchs lives in West Berlin with his wife Heidi and daughter Suzanne. They share a cosy small house with a large black tom cat called Paul. Heidi works as a librarian, while Wolfgang is the proprietor of two drug stores in the shopping centre of Neukolln. At weekends the family sail a yacht on the Wannsee, which they share with a number of individuals, most of whom were once connected to Wolfgang's 'firm' in some way – either as workers or clients for his services. He officially 'retired' from the escape business in 1973, for the simple reason that he had to build up an existence for his family and attend to the matter of earning a living. Wolfgang Fuchs cannot remember how many refugees he has helped but a conservative estimate would put the total number at over five hundred. Among those in the know in West Berlin, he is a living legend, nicknamed 'Tunnel Fuchs', and the DDR would probably love to get their hands on him – for which reason he always leaves the city by air and never uses the transit autobahn. If the family need their car on holiday in the West, it has to be driven to Hannover by a courier.

In 1961, the young Wolfgang was a political idealist, leaning like many young Germans towards the right, and most certainly anti-Communist. From his youth he remembered the privations of the blockade and the constant tension in the divided city. He lived in the West, with his then wife, Selina, in the East; a typical Berlin relationship of the pre-Wall period. Indeed, the first escape he organised was to bring his wife over a few days after 13 August 1961, before the defences had become properly established. From then until his retirement he was to be fully occupied with the Wall out of idealism rather than profit – an activity that cost him his first marriage but also brought its rewards in a personal sense of achievement. He is proud of the escapes he organised and of the friendship of many of those he helped. He is a large man, generous, warm-hearted and outgoing. Born in another time, he would have been a successful soldier, perhaps in a commando-type unit, where he could match his courage with meticulous planning. In German his name means fox, which was singularly appropriate for the man who was probably the greatest escape organiser of them all.

Like most of his contemporaries, Wolfgang Fuchs slithered into the escape business by accident, through having a relative (his wife) who had to be helped. Also, he knew a lot of students who were to become the mainstay of the early period. Many of their comrades came from the East and had attended the West Berlin universities quite freely, but then one day there were empty places in the lecture halls and laboratories. Friends were missing and anguished messages asking for help were passed through the Wall. Girlfriends were smuggled over in the early days of simple barbed wire, but soon after it was necessary to explore more complicated methods.

Fuchs, young and active, became a focus for the student groups. West Germans, as opposed to West Berliners, were always able to cross over to the East on a day pass. These were comparatively easy to forge but the success was short-lived. The DDR introduced new currency exchange certificates with a duplicate sheet which had to be left at the checkpoint on entry. When the visitor left, the duplicate was compared with the one in his or her possession, and a switch of identity would have been discovered. So Fuchs started his underground career by examining the sewerage system which ran under the Wall at several places. No sooner had he worked out the possibilities than the East Germans fitted solid metal grilles across the tunnels and coupled them to sensitive alarms. He was forced back to finding ways over the Wall, and in the process got to know every metre of the frontier as he and a small circle of friends constantly patrolled along it looking for possibilities. The problem was that such individual actions could only help one or at the most two refugees at any one time. A tunnel on the other hand, if undiscovered for any length of time, offered the chance of bringing over a whole group.

In a space of about two years, in 1963 and 1964, Wolfgang Fuchs built no less than seven tunnels under the Wall. The first ones were comparatively short and simple, as at that time the authorities in the East had not started to demolish houses on their side of the border and had not established the prohibited zone or the wide death strip. The method was to gain access to the cellar of a house in the West and dig through 20 or 30 metres to a cellar on the opposite side. By the end of the period, however, the length of tunnel had increased to some 130 metres, with electric lighting, artificial ventilation and vast quantities of timber required for shoring the walls. As anybody knows who has read of escapes by tunnel from prison camps during the war, the main difficulty is disposal of the excavated soil, which is a terrible giveaway – the longer the tunnel the more earth you have to hide. In addition, a much larger crew is needed, working in shifts, who have to be fed and housed.

Finance was a perennial problem but in the early days there were those prepared to step into the breach. Supporters ranged from right-wing political parties such as the Christian Democrats and anti-Communist organisations, to wealthy private individuals who donated money or goods. The media too was a source to be tapped, especially the Berlin-based Springer newspaper chain and such magazines as *Stern*. Fuchs made the point that had he not been able to raise the money for the tunnels, he would have had to take money from the refugees themselves. Also in those early days he was able to rely on a high degree of official support which ranged from tacit toleration to active help from the police. He said that he and his helpers armed themselves with a variety of ancient guns to protect themselves both while in a tunnel and from assassination attempts by East German agents when on the surface. One day they were visited by a West Berlin police inspector who saw their arsenal and promptly confiscated their weapons as being potentially unsafe. But the following day he returned with a supply of modern pistols and a stock of ammunition.

The Fuchs organisation was known at the time as 'Klunte and Klunte'. He himself was known as Klunte One, and Klunte Two was a brilliant young university lecturer called Reinhard Furrer. For years the latter dropped out of the limelight while making a career as an academic, but in the autumn of 1985 his escape-helping career once more received prominence when he was selected as West Germany's first astronaut for a trip in the Space Shuttle. The reason for the media interest was concerned with the tragic end of the tunnelling period which will shortly be discussed.

At the time, there were several tunnelling groups in action, one comprising a number of Italian students financed by the US television company NBC. Fuchs himself built two long tunnels, both from the Bernauerstrasse through to the Strelitzerstrasse. The first one was a failure as its existence had been discovered by the police in the East. They were nearly ready to make the breakthrough and, luckily for all concerned, the team had retired to the cellar base at the Western end for a very necessary part of the operation. The actual breakthrough was always the most dangerous and nerve-racking part of tunnel-building. You never knew whether the coast would be clear or whether you would be looking into the muzzle of a Kalashinikov. The team were constructing a scarecrow mounted on the end of a pole which they intended to poke up through, when suddenly they were simply blown flat by the blast wave of a massive explosion. The East Germans had managed to dig down into the tunnel and had thrown a bomb into it. Fuchs reckons that if he had been caught in the shaft his lungs would have been ruptured by the pressure. The danger of betrayal or discovery was ever present, especially in an environment where there was no clearly defined enemy. Germany divided was and still is a nation with divided loyalties, and in Berlin, the joke is that half the citizens are spying on the other half. Rivals in the escape business tended at times to betray their competitors, and the East German secret police had a swarm of informants in the West. For Fuchs and his team, security became an obsession. No potential refugee was accepted unless introduced by someone known to the organisation. When tunnelling, the workers were housed on site to minimise the coming and going, and when someone had to leave the building, this was done at night and using a back door.

The last Fuchs tunnel became known as 'Tunnel 57', because on the nights of 3–5 October 1964, 57 people were brought through. It was 130 metres long and took a team of forty helpers six months to build. Finance was provided by a magazine and by the aid of a film made during the work and on the actual night of the escape. Fuchs managed to obtain the use of a bakery in the Bernauerstrasse which was due to be demolished. On the other side his couriers found suitable premises in the Strelitzerstrasse. These were empty blocks of apartments, the inhabitants of which had been forced to move, because of their proximity to the Wall. The team moved into the bakery and from the cellar they sank a shaft 3 metres down to tunnel level. This was fitted with a hoist for lifting up the buckets of soil which were then emptied in the spare cellar rooms. By the time they had finished the entire cellar and the ground-floor rooms were all packed solid with earth.

The author asked Fuchs about the feeling of working underground, making slow but steady progress towards the East. He thought for a moment and then replied:

I believe that I have seldom been so happy in my life, however corny that may sound, than when I was down there, I always sang…. When one is underground for ten days under the Wall and drills and digs, and another cubic metre of earth has been cleared, one gets another step forward. That is a dreamlike feeling really. I mean that seriously.

Typical of the cheekiness and humour of the team, when the line of the tunnel actually came to the frontier they put up a notice similar to the ones to be seen all over Berlin: 'You are leaving the American Sector.' Fuchs himself may have been happy when digging, but that should not disguise the days of sheer backbreaking toil cramped in the narrow shaft, breathing in the bad air and with the ever present fear of flooding or a roof collapse. All that calls for courage of a particular kind.

They were not like prisoners seeking escape for themselves, but were working to help others escape, for no personal reward other than their keep and a limited amount of pocket money.

When the tunnel was finally finished, the refugees had to be assembled as unobtrusively as possible. West Germans who could freely move about in East Berlin acted as the couriers. One of the selected group was Dieter Thaelmann, a 29-year-old engineer who had served a sentence as a political prisoner in the East. He received a coded telegram at his home in Dresden, warning him to be ready, and made his way to East Berlin. On arrival he went to the Friedrichstrasse station and looked at the timetable with interest. What followed was pure Le Carré. After a few minutes he was joined by a stranger, who placed his finger over the large letter D for Dresden on the notice board. Without looking round, Thaelmann whispered the password, which was 'Tokyo', the site of the Olympic games that year. The stranger strolled off and Thaelmann followed some distance behind. After a while the man in front stopped and asked for a light, which was the excuse for a whispered conversation before they parted. Thaelmann was told to make his way to No. 55 Strelitzerstrasse and when he turned into the street he was under observation from the West. Wolfgang Fuchs was on the roof of a house which overlooked the East, equipped with binoculars and a radio transmitter. When he was satisfied that the escaper did not have a 'tail', he called up his helpers in the apartment block and gave them permission to open the door. Thaelmann rang the bell, gave the password and was admitted. Once inside he was taken across a courtyard, down some stairs into the cellar where there was a bathroom with an old wooden crate in the middle. This was pushed aside to reveal the entrance to the shaft, and eleven minutes later, after a crawl on hands and knees, he was in the West.

In this and similar ways, a total of fity-seven refugees were brought to the tunnel entrance and through the damp dark passage on hands and knees to freedom. Once they had arrived in the cellar at the Bernauerstrasse, their identity was carefully checked to establish that they were genuine. This was followed by a thorough cleaning-up session. The Fuchs organisation provided buckets of water to wash off any traces of mud because the last thing they wanted was for a whole stream of grubby strangers to be let loose on the West Berlin streets at the dead of night. Their clients were kept in quarantine in the cellar for anything up to six hours before being released in small unobtrusive groups.

Talking to the author in 1986, Wolfgang Fuchs remembered those particular nights in terms of happiness.

> I must say that the most beautiful feeling was for me to see when the people came crawling out of the tunnel, on their knees from East Berlin like mice. I can never forget. The marks of their knee prints in the tunnel floor looked like the ripples on a beach left behind by the receding tide. It does not matter what may become of me, I will never forget that. That is beautiful and that is happiness.

Looking at the photographs taken in that cellar one of those nights, it is perhaps easier to understand just what he meant. One man embraces the wife from whom he had been separated by the Wall for three years. In order to be reunited he had helped to build the tunnel. Another man had spent every weekend working on the project, from Friday evening to Monday morning. His reward was when his brother crawled through. A young girl was simply told by her parents that they were going for a stroll, so as to save her the fear that the rest of the family felt. Her 'stroll' also ended in freedom and the chance to see her grandmother again.

But then disaster struck. Very early in the morning of 5 October 1964, four students were still at the Eastern end of the tunnel in the Strelitzerstrasse house and were armed with pistols. They carried these with the intention only of using them to fire a warning shot if there was an emergency, before bolting back down the tunnel. Just after midnight two men dressed in civilian clothes came to the door which led into the courtyard of the apartment block. Although they did not know the password, they looked so scared that the students foolishly assumed that the men were genuine refugees and let them in. They were then told to take off their shoes so as to be able to cross the yard silently. One did so, but the other begged to be allowed to go and collect a friend who was hiding nearby and had lost his nerve. The students intended to let only one of them go but then the other said that they had come so far together and did not want to be separated. So they were both allowed to leave, in a clear breach of the normal security precautions. The students were fully aware that if three returned they were probably genuine refugees, and anyway, the men had seen that two of the students were carrying their weapons openly.

After about a quarter of an hour, the two returned with a third man. The fact that the latter was in uniform was not immediately noticed because of the darkness. The helper standing in the door was told that he was under arrest and the civilians ordered the man in uniform to take off the safety catch on his machine pistol. He then moved forward into the courtyard threatening the student with his weapon, while the two civilians, who were almost certainly State Security men, remained in the background. It seemed to those who were there that the soldier was very unsure of himself and had not been properly briefed as to what to expect. Seeing the hopeless position of his friend, one of the other students who was in the courtyard fired a warning shot to give his friend the chance to reach the tunnel entrance. Immediately the soldier opened fire and this was returned by the student who aimed at the muzzle flash, firing seven shots. Then a fusillade opened up from all directions – seemingly the courtyard was surrounded. Ducking and weaving, the two students ran into the building which housed the tunnel entrance and bolted to safety.

Subsequently it was revealed that the soldier, whose name was Egon Schultz, died, and naturally the East German press made a propaganda field day out of the affair, accusing Western fascist elements of having murdered him. It remains to this day unclear whether he was hit by one of the random shots fired by an untrained student with a pistol and who was running at the time, or whether Schultz was caught in the cross-fire of his own people. Had it been a bullet of pistol calibre the authorities in the East would undoubtedly have been more than happy to produce the evidence, but they never did. Naturally they demanded the extradition of those responsible, which was not granted, and the students maintained that they had acted in self-defence. One of the two young men in the courtyard that night was 'Klunte 2', Reinhard Furrer the astronaut, whose part in the affair was raked up again in West German magazines in 1985.

This event effectively ended Fuch's tunnel-building activities. The authorities in the West started to look with disfavour at the efforts of the escape helpers, as they were more concerned with doing a deal with East Germany to grant day passes for West Berliners to visit their relatives in the East of the divided city. Besides, the East Germans were busily demolishing whole rows of houses and blocks of flats that backed on to the frontier to create a wide death strip and prohibited zone. Patrols in the latter were stepped up and anyone considered remotely unreliable was forcibly moved to an area well away from the Wall. Only Party members and armed forces personnel remained anywhere near the border, and without a safe entrance in the East, tunnel-building was a waste of time.

Even in the tunnel period, however, Fuchs was alive to other possibilities and one day read an article about the escape of the train robber Ronald Biggs from Wandsworth Prison in England. In this famous operation, a furniture lorry was driven alongside the wall of the exercise yard of Wandsworth Prison. Helpers pushed ladders over, and Biggs plus three others scrambled over, down through a hole in the roof of the lorry and out at the back, to the waiting getaway cars. Fuchs reasoned that he could try a similar stunt. The story of the cemetery escape is a classic tale of the ingenuity employed by 'Klunte and Klunte'.

Living in East Berlin was a 25-year-old engineer named Jurgen Kummer who was in love with a girl called Gisela Meyer – who happened to live in West Germany. The two had met at a birthday party in the East, which Gisela as a West German could freely visit. Normally their love would have been frustrated by the existence of the Wall unless Gisela had been prepared to move to a drab existence as a citizen of the DDR, but she was related to a senior person working for one of the leading West German magazines – which had already done business with Wolfgang Fuchs. He was approached and agreed to collect Jurgen, although at that stage he did not have any fixed plan in mind. He sent a courier through to the East, checked the young man out and told him to wait for further instructions. Still fascinated by the Biggs escape, Fuchs began to make daily tours of the Wall in a secondhand Volkswagen minibus which had been donated by a well-wisher. On one of these trips he ended up in the Liesenstrasse in the French sector to the north of the city centre. In early 1965, the wall of the cemetery marked the border and had not been replaced by today's concrete monstrosity, and from a vantage point he observed that people were still permitted into the cemetery itself to tend the graves. *Grepos* patrolled the narrow strip of grass immediately behind the wall, at the foot of which were rolls of coiled barbed wire. Further research revealed that special passes were needed to enter the cemetery, but that Jurgen had an aunt buried there. With the help of a minister in the East, such a pass was obtained and Jurgen began regular Sunday visits to establish a pattern of behaviour.

On the other side, Fuchs rented a third-floor flat in the Liesenstrasse directly overlooking the cemetery and for six months observed the pattern of the guards' routine. In addition, he noticed that there was a patch of dead ground where a chapel obstructed the view from a watchtower, which would cover a running person for twenty seconds. It was this which determined his choice of the point for the escape. Fuchs obtained a small lorry and had a special hinged ladder made to be poked over the Wall and then unfolded so as to drop down over the coils of barbed wire on the other side. The signal that all was ready was to be the opening of a lace curtain in the third-floor flat.

In order to extract maximum publicity from the escape, a local cameraman, Helmut Sonntag, was permitted to film from the flat, and the pictures he shot remain one of the most fascinating documents of the early period of the Wall. Jurgen was briefed by yet another courier and for four Sundays in a row, equipped with fresh flowers, a rake and a watering can, the young man made his way to the cemetery. Kneeling at the grave to replace the flowers, he watched for the signal, nerves tensed to make the dash, but the curtain remained closed. He had to return home fighting down the tension inside himself and trying to look normal as he showed his pass at the gate.

On the fifth Sunday, conditions were perfect. The watcher at the window noted that the guards were at the far end of their beat, and that as it was lunchtime, there were few other mourners about. He pulled aside the curtain, and Jurgen, noticing this, began to move as nonchalantly as he could towards the Wall. On the other side, in the street, Fuchs started the engine of his lorry and raced towards the spot, backing hard up against the Wall. His helpers pushed the ladder up and with a broomstick struggled frantically to poke the hinged part over. As this finally crashed over, Jurgen saw it, dropped the watering can and rake, and ran for his life. Seen through the eye of Helmut Sonntag's camera, Jurgen grasped the bottom part of the ladder and started to climb up and was then pulled over the crest of the Wall, as the *Grepos* shouted at him to stop. He tumbled into the back of the lorry which then moved away from the Wall, while those on board jumped up and down hugging each other and the refugee with relief and excitement. Then Fuch's first wife Selina ran up and jumped on board to join the prancing group, as a West German police van arrived on the scene.

In the East, the post-mortem began. Soon the cemetery was full of uniformed and plain clothes police, stumbling around among the graves looking for clues, and the necessary conclusions were drawn. Within weeks, observers in the West noticed workmen exhuming all the graves within 30 metres of the Wall to create a death strip and putting up an inner wall. Standing at the window of that same flat today the scene is quite different. A standard outer wall topped by concrete pipes, a smoothly raked earth strip, signal wires and a patrol road. Beyond this a plain whitewashed inner wall and only then the remaining area of cemetery.

For Fuchs, however, the first heady days were already past. As early as December 1963, the West German counter-intelligence people had discovered one of his tunnels and had forbidden him to carry on with the work. His telephone was tapped, and the authorities wanted nothing to disturb their negotiations for Christmas passes for West Berliners to visit the East. He even got arrested and charged with 'illegal crossing of a political demarcation line' when he tried to fly leaflets over to the East with a helium-filled balloon. At that same period, he had thought up a new version of the Trojan Horse. The plan was to hoist a large metal water tank over the wall with a crane, the sides of which were thick enough to withstand machine-pistol rounds. Six refugees would then jump in and be lifted to safety. The West Berlin police knew about the attempt and ordered Fuchs to desist, even sending a messenger with an official court order, which Fuchs ignored. He had hired a crane and the driver practised with a section of replica wall they had built on a bombsite, timing his lift against a stopwatch. Then the authorities struck. They confiscated the crane, justifying their action by claiming that it was standing where parking was not allowed. To this day, Wolfgang Fuchs is bitter about this and the political motivation for stopping his activities. Police harassment meant yet another change of tactics, as he decided that he would not let himself be intimidated. Like other escape helpers, he came to the realisation that the period of spectacular attempts over or under the Wall was at an end. The Eastern defences had become too sophisticated and the political goodwill in the West was at an end. There was contact at ministerial level between the two Germanys and after years of stagnation trade was beginning to blossom. Only a few years afterwards, Willi Brandt, the hero of Berlin, would visit Willi Stoph, the Minister President of the DDR, and tacit recognition would be accorded to the regime that permitted its officials to shoot refugees on the Wall.

Fuchs turned his attention to cars and those entitled to cross legitimately. All normal cars were meticulously searched for hidden compartments, mirrors were placed underneath and papers were examined with minute care – as a result of the various spectacular escapes discussed previously. There was, however, one category of cross-border traveller not subject to such attention: diplomats accredited to the DDR who preferred to do their shopping in West Berlin. Fuchs discovered through his contacts a Syrian diplomat who was hard up and did not even own a car, but was very keen to have a Mercedes. The

Fuchs organisation naturally enough were more than willing to oblige with a suitable vehicle, secondhand so as not to excite too much curiosity. The Syrian, in return, undertook a whole series of runs through Checkpoint Charlie with refugees in the boot.

It was at this juncture, in 1965, that a certain young lady in East Berlin was brought to the notice of the Fuchs organisation, as being somebody worthy of being helped. In her late teens, Heidi had manufactured crude anti-regime leaflets with a child's printing kit and had started to circulate them in East Berlin. Inevitably she was caught and sentenced to two years in prison for anti-state propaganda. After serving her sentence in degrading conditions she was unable to work as a professional librarian but had good friends, one of whom came over from the West to visit her. Heidi was simply told that she would be helped and that a courier would be in contact, called Klaus, if a man, or Karin if a woman. She waited several weeks and then received a telephone call from 'Klaus' who said that another person would be in touch fairly shortly. This second contact ordered her to be at a certain spot in East Berlin on a certain date, where she met up with a young man who was to be her companion on the attempt. Their courier gave them orders on military lines: 'When I tell you to turn around then you turn around, and when I say run into the field, then you run into that, and when I say down you throw yourselves down. When I say jump you will find an open car boot waiting for you and into that you jump.' Sure enough the open car boot was there and the two escapees jumped in. Heidi remembers being crammed into the small space with the young man and the nerve-racking drive in the dark. Then the car stopping, voices of the guards outside and the engine restarting. The car moved slowly off and then zig-zagged through the obstacles just before the actual frontier. Only when the car drove straight again did Heidi realise that she was safe, and a few minutes later the boot was opened – by a strange young man who helped them out. That was Wolfgang Fuchs. The years of tunnelling and plotting had taken their toll of his marriage, which by then was on the rocks. He was divorced and subsequently married Heidi, who became an accepted member of his team.

That was the second run undertaken by the Syrian diplomat. He made many more but inevitably, as always seems to happen in Berlin, he was betrayed. Fuchs was waiting at Checkpoint Charlie and saw what happened. Just before entering the checkpoint, the car was surrounded by State Security police, who dragged the Syrian out at gunpoint, and then went for the boot. A whole family was hidden inside and they too were taken away. The Syrian could not be arrested as such as he had diplomatic immunity, but he was interrogated for several days and then declared persona non grata. From the cells of the State Security he was put on an 'Interflug' aircraft for Syria where sentence of death awaited him. Fuchs, however, looked after his people and had provided the man with a good set of false papers, which he was able to use when the aircraft stopped at Rome to refuel. Eight weeks later and knowing that the Syrian was safe, Wolfgang and Heidi went off to Spain on honeymoon, but heard on a short-wave broadcast that the whole story had broken. Fearful of political repercussions they hurriedly packed their bags and returned to Berlin.

With the diplomatic car no longer available, other methods had to be considered as the team were still obsessed with outwitting the East German authorities. Berlin itself had by then become too hot and every innocent citizen was a potential enemy agent. Even today it is a common joke that there is no such thing as a secure telephone in the city, and the visiting journalist putting up at a hotel is almost certain to have his room searched at some point in his stay. By them or us? One never knows.

The answer that had occurred to others in the business was to use other frontiers – between Czechoslovakia or Hungary and Austria for example, or even Romania into Turkey. Refugees were instructed to travel on holiday to another Eastern bloc country and there they were contacted by a courier. The age-old tricks of secret compartments and petrol tanks divided in half were soon outplayed. As his final gamble before retirement, Fuchs and his helpers spent six months perfecting 'Supercar'. It was never suspected, made a considerable number of runs and the author has promised not to reveal its secret. All that can be said is that it was a large American vehicle that could be subjected to the most rigorous search including virtual demolition at a frontier post, and that the hiding place was most uncomfortable and cramped for the person within. The car still exists and is in honourable retirement at a secret location somewhere in West Germany. Who knows, it might have to be used once again in a worthy cause.

Twenty-five years after the building of the Wall and fourteen years after his 'retirement', Wolfgang Fuchs is philosophical about the past but still angry over the very existence of the Wall. While others of his age group had been building up their careers he had been helping refugees to escape and is still furious if accused of having profited from his activities. I asked him why he had chosen to act as he did.

Well, it was a career for me and it was fun to do. After all, I might have needed help myself and it could have cost me my life. I found so many friends, quite spontaneously, to whom I was unable to give any guarantees. It was fun to help and I would do it again and again – I believe that all our friends who worked with us would do it again. It was not a negative period for us, but a positive time – it enriched our lives.

Again on the theme of happiness, he spoke about the frequent vigils at Checkpoint Charlie.

Happiness is when you see a car coming five hundred metres before the checkpoint and you see the headlights moving up and down because you know there is weight in the boot. You know that no soul can help you and that there are people hidden in there who want to get away and don't want to be shot. Then the sweat breaks out on your forehead as it drives into the checkpoint and the driver shows his pass. Everything OK and the car moves off towards you. That is dreamlike happiness.

Anchored in the West German constitution is the right to live where one wishes, which naturally is in conflict with those who today seek accommodation with the DDR, at almost any price. Fuchs does not deny the need for contact between the two Germanys, but even so feels a sense of betrayal.

> If we deny our constitution, a democratic one which was given to us by the Allies after the war, if we throw that overboard and say that those who want to flee no longer have the right to come over here anymore, then I would not understand the world. I must be able to say that this is right and this is not right. I must be allowed to help a person who wants to get away from there and come over here, who has the right under our constitution – there is no doubt about that.

In a final comment he went on to express the hope that one day the Wall would be demolished by a gradual thaw in East–West rigidity and drew a parallel between the Berlin problem and the situation in Alsace-Lorraine today. That bitterly fought-over territory, for centuries the bone of contention between European powers, is now at peace. Its people can speak either French or German and move easily across the borders.

If ever in the future there is one man who will become associated in the mind of history with the Berlin Wall and escapes then that must surely be Wolfgang Fuchs, to whom so many owe so much and who gave all he had to help.

18. *East German guards survey bomb damage in the Wall caused by western protesters.*

19. *East German guards cocking a snook at western spectators.*

20. *President Kennedy at the Brandenburg Gate in June 1963, escorted by the Mayor of Berlin, Willi Brandt, and Chancellor Konrad Adenauer. The arches of the Gate were draped in red banners to stop East Germans from watching their visit.*

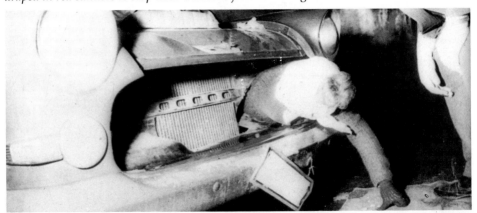

21. *Eighteen refugees escaped from East Berlin in this car.*

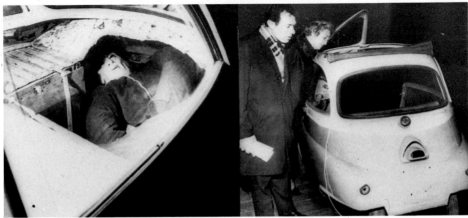

22. *This Isetta made several successful trips through the Wall.*

23. *The Austin-Healey Sprite used by Hans Peter Meixner.*

24. *Two successful escapes were made in this cable drum, which could carry four people. The third escape was betrayed.*

25. *Above: Ilse Hewitt in East Berlin.*

26. *Above right: the driver of this bus tried to ram through the Wall unsuccessfully. Several of his passengers were hurt.*

27. *Right: the Hewitts in London, after their escape.*

6

The Idealists

Wolfgang Fuchs was not the only idealist marooned in a world that was to become more and more dominated by purely commercial motives and ultimately by downright criminality. As the Wall became an established fact of life in Berlin and it dawned on people that it was not just a temporary construction put up by the East German authorities, so the escape-helping organisations developed of their own accord. While some brave people in the East were lucky enough to dream up and carry through their own plans, others needed the help of outsiders. We have seen that the students were involved early on, helping fellow students come over to the West. Others helped their relatives out and they found a taste for the danger and excitement. They were often the sort of people who during a war tend to make their mark in elite units – individualists who are difficult to assimilate into the mass anonymity of a regiment or battalion. As West Berliners were unable to cross over to the Eastern side of the city, many of those who became involved had West German papers or had to use couriers who were either West Germans or foreigners.

   The morality of escape helping had long been a matter of discussion in German books and newspaper articles, and the moralists argue that it is wrong to accept money from people for assisting them to flee to the West. In the beginning of the Wall period it was fairly simple to be high-minded, as there were plenty of sources of finance available to the helpers: the right-wing press, anti-Communist pressure groups, conservative political parties and motivated individuals. They paid the expenses and the living costs of various groups of young-sters who were not living in luxury anyway. As the defences along the Wall strengthened, reliance had to be placed on technical gadgetry. It was one thing to forge a simple pass or to hustle someone out in the boot of a car, and quite another thing to prepare a secret hiding place or to spend six months digging a tunnel. Expert help had to be hired, workshops found, timber and tools obtained, and so on. Another matter that had to be taken into account was the risk factor. Once people realised that their lives were in danger or that at best, if captured they were likely to spend up to eight years in prison, so the stock of volunteers for courier work began to dry up. If people could be found to make runs into the East with the ever present danger of betrayal and capture, they naturally demanded some sort of fee commensurate with the degree of danger to which they would be exposed. This tended to let in the professionals who had an eye on the financial possibilities and so the price of help rose dramatically through the 1960s. Today, we are told, the fees for bringing out a family through Hungary or one of the other Eastern bloc states are in the region of 100,000 DM. In the early 1960s the price of the trip over the wall was nearer 1500 DM.

The author would certainly maintain that it is essentially immoral to make a rich living out of the misery of others and simply to exploit their natural desire to live in freedom. Many of the professionals ended up as wealthy men, owning res-taurants in Berlin and villas in Spain. Against this can be argued that they ran the risk, but this is not true. It was the refugees who ran the risk together with underlings who were paid a fee as couriers, while the organisers remained safely in the West. It was those who charged only expenses and a modest fee to cover their living costs while working on the escape who could be termed idealists, and a few are still operating today.

Many of the youngsters who went into escape helping in the early years paid for their efforts with their lives or with long spells in prison, often through innocence or lack of experience. Others ended up as victims of chance. Dieter Wohlfahrt was a twenty-year-old student who without profit to himself had managed to get more than fifty people through the early wire defences. One day he was approached by a girl who pleaded with him to help her mother to escape, and foolishly he seems to have made no effort to check up on them. He simply ignored the safety precautions used by the Fuchs organisation, of only taking on refugees who were personally vouched for. He worked out a route through the wire at Staaken, which lies to the west of the ring around Berlin, and told the girl to ensure that her mother would be waiting there concealed close to the border. At the agreed time he arrived, received the correct signal from the mother and began stealthily to cut through the wire, without any suspicion. He was quite unaware that guards were waiting in hiding for him and as soon as he started work they opened fire without any warning. He fell mortally wounded, with the girl watching.

A few weeks later a frontier guard whose name was Heinz Kleim fled to the East out of shame for what had happened. He told his interrogators that two hours before Wohlfahrt was shot, the mother had been present at their company head-quarters and that they had all known of what was going to happen that day in December 1961. Another who paid with his life was Siegfried Noffke. Cut off in the West of the city as a result of the Wall he naturally wanted to bring out his wife and their baby. Gathering together a band of helpers he decided on a tunnel and set to work from the basement of a house in the Heidelbergerstrasse, the scene of several of the early tunnels. This was a natural place to choose as the frontier ran right down the middle of the street with tall houses on either side. Today this is one of the few places in Berlin where the houses in the East have not been demolished and where one can still get an impression of the conditions when the Wall was first built. Noffke and his friends dug away busily and were soon over the border, a distance of not more than 30 metres, but unknown to them, a group of students were also tunnelling from the neighbouring cellar. Their efforts caused an earth slip which alarmed the East German police and resulted in a thorough search and a well-planned ambush. When Noffke was ready, he and two helpers went through the tunnel, equipped with a car jack to force a way through the floor of a cellar in the East. The pressure of the jack broke through the floor and Noffke climbed out only to be shot on sight. His two helpers were arrested and sentenced to prison for life.

Life became established as the standard penalty for helping people to escape, although that was not mentioned when charges were framed. Those caught were regarded as terrorists by the authorities in the DDR. One of the first to escape over the Wall in the late summer of 1961 was Harry Seidel, a man in his mid-twenties who had been the East German cycling champion. For a little over a year he became a one-man crusader against the East German regime, constantly dreaming up plans to bring others out, including his wife and baby. Tragedy first struck when he tried to collect his mother, who was caught and sentenced to eighteen months in prison for attempting to flee the republic. Seidel is credited with having helped more than forty people to escape and was involved with several of the early tunnels which he helped to dig himself. It would seem that he was motivated by a need for revenge, but drifted into unsavoury company, teaming up with two professionals, one of whom had a criminal record. On 14 November 1962 he had finished a tunnel in the Kleinmachow area of West Berlin and made his breakthrough, only to be ambushed and captured. When he was put on trial in East Germany, great emphasis was placed on the fact that when caught he had been armed with a pistol. In the judge's summing up he stated:

> Seidel and other members of terrorist organisations forced their way a considerable number of times into the territory of the German Democratic Republic via underground tunnels, armed with loaded pistols and sub-machine guns, whereby they kidnapped citizens of the said republic. The crimes committed by the accused are a representation of the aggressive and militaristic policies of the Bonn government and the Senate of West Berlin, which threaten to plunge the world into the catastrophe of the third world war fought with atomic bombs and missiles. This state-organised systematic undermining of the state border of the D.D.R. is thus aggression and preparation for war.

The unfortunate Seidel was sentenced to life imprisonment and immediately a campaign to demand his freedom developed in the West. Along the Wall, Berliners demonstrated with placards and banners, watched by guards from the East, and a twenty-four hour fast was organised. One of the banners made the point that helping someone to escape was only re-establishing a basic right. In the event, he only served four years. He was ransomed by the Bonn government for the sum of 30,000 DM and deported to the West where he was able to join his wife and child. Even his mother was released, as after serving her sentence she had reached pensionable age and was entitled to leave legally.

In the museum at Checkpoint Charlie there is a photograph showing a man and a small boy in the corridor of a flat. The man is wearing a white shirt and striped trousers and the boy has a rather astonished look on his face. This was taken after their escape and the father is demonstrating a self-made harness of webbing straps fixed to a roller. The man is Gerhard Moessner and the boy is his 9-year-old son. Just to the south of the Potzdamerplatz where the tourist coaches stop to enable visitors to peer over the Wall and buy souvenirs, there is a large imposing stone building quite close to the frontier. This is known as the 'House of Ministries' and is occupied by various official DDR government bodies. During the Second World War it was Hermann Goering's Air Ministry and its architecture is typical of the Third Reich style which, but for the activities of the Allied bomber fleets, would have totally changed the face of the city. It has five storeys and a low pitched roof. Gerhard Moessner, in his mid-thirties at the time, was employed there as a maintenance fitter and although content with his job, was daily confronted by the view of the West from the windows. One of his special responsibilities was the care of the lift mechanism which often took him on to the roof and it was while up there that he had the idea, having seen the chair lifts in ski resorts. He had a number of friends in the West, one of whom was a West German student, and he discussed his plan with this young man, who agreed to get together a team of helpers.

Moessner went to work on his preparations stealthily, and as a fitter had the necessary tools and access to materials. Firstly he constructed on top of the building a metal stand that was solid enough to take a considerable weight, and then secreted a spare lift cable which he passed to his student friend for smuggling out to the West. His wife got busy and sewed the necessary harnesses for the three of them. On the day planned for the escape attempt, he smuggled his wife and son into the building and locked them in a small toilet, and when the day's work was over he hid himself until everyone had left. Shortly after midnight, everything was ready and the family stood out on the roof in the biting cold wind of a winter night. Below them they could see the brightly floodlit death strip, the Wall, and beyond, the lights of West Berlin where they hoped that their helpers were ready. The latter had taken up position on a patch of waste ground close to the Wall, and one of them managed to short circuit the floodlights. As these dimmed and flickered out, a signal was flashed by torch to the roof and Moessner heaved a hammer coated with luminous paint over the Wall to the waiting students. Attached to the end of this was a length of nylon fishing line. They found the gently glowing hammer in the darkness and attached the steel cable to the fishing line which Moessner then pulled up to the roof. It must have been an immense physical effort but he managed it and made the hawser fast to the anchorpoint.

His wife was the first to go. She was absolutely terrified as her roller was slipped over the cable while she clung to the parapet. Then she had to let go and disappeared into the darkness. Sweeping down over the Wall she was grabbed by unknown hands as she hit the ground and slipped out of her harness. On the roof her husband felt the cable go slack and hooked on his son. Lifting the slight little boy he dropped him over the edge. Once again he felt the sudden release of the weight and hooked himself on his own trip. He seemed secure as the speed built up but there was an alarming drop as the tension in the cable began to sag. The students on the other end who were holding the cable tight were almost at the end of their strength and Moessner brushed the top of the wire with his feet as he swept down to collapse before them. A whole family had dared and won, and all that was left for the guards the following morning was to recover the cable.

Walter Jacobsen was only 17 in August 1961 but was soon

involved in helping people across the Wall. He brought out two girls with the help of a group of students who staged a demonstration to distract the attention of the guards. This success attracted publicity and Jacobsen was named in the newspapers as the person responsible, being cited as a hero. This he undoubtedly was but his cover was blown. One of the girls had left her two small children behind and after only two weeks in West Berlin decided, apparently of her own free will, to return to the East. There she quickly came to the notice of the authorities and was probably put under pressure by the State Security police. At any rate she signed a deposition complaining that she had been abducted forcibly and taken to the West against her wishes. Jacobsen's extradition was demanded on a charge of kidnapping but naturally he was not handed over or even charged in the West. His fate, however, had been sealed. Just after Christmas 1961, an East German agent knocked at his door and asked for help, explaining that his sister wanted to escape. Jacobsen agreed to assist and nominated a rendezvous close to the border, but when he met his contact there, armed guards appeared and he was dragged into East Berlin. Once in prison there the authorities bided their time, holding him for eight months until he was 18 and could be tried as an adult. Yet oddly enough he got away with a four year sentence and was released back to West Berlin towards the end of 1965.

Finally in this chapter is the heartwarming story of Harry Kalbowski, whose career was a remarkable one. He was one of the early swimmers who made it across the Teltow Canal and had taken great care in his attempt. In the dark he had crawled through the wire, cutting the lower strands as he went and carefully rejoining them behind him. To his surprise he discovered that the guards did not stumble upon his route and that their view from a watchtower was partially screened by the high bank of the canal. His security was good and he only contacted people from his home town, Gera, whom he knew wanted to escape. For the best part of the year he regularly swam the freezing waters of the canal, opened up the passage through the wire and shepherded his friends across. In one six-week period he was able to help twelve escapees and even managed to save two children by holding their heads above water as he swam with them. His luck ran out in December 1962 when he was discovered by a patrol trying to bring out an entire family, the head of which was shot. Kalbowski himself was put on trial for inducing people to defect and was sentenced to four and a half years penal servitude. That, however, was not a deterrent and in the summer of 1963 he escaped from Gera Prison and naturally enough made his way back to his favourite spot on the Teltow Canal. En route he was recaptured and transferred to another more secure prison. Yet it would seem that the East German authorities did not take his break-out too amiss for the following year he was released on appeal, because he could prove that he had never taken any money from those he had helped. The problem was that when the prison door was opened, as an ex-citizen of the DDR he was sent back to Gera and was not permitted to settle in the West. In January 1965 (like a homing pigeon), he was back in the canal on a night when the water temperature was six degrees under freezing point, it was pitch dark and the guards were not looking for swimmers. Quietly he slid into the water for the last time and made his way across to the West Berlin shore. Once in safety his fertile mind was occupied with further efforts to help others, but fate intervened when he was killed in a car accident, putting an end to the career of a man who had achieved so much.

7

The Professionals

In the previous chapter we saw how a need was created for assistance in helping others to escape and how, inevitably, money began to play a role. The early idealists were compared to resistance fighters during the war by the then deputy mayor of West Berlin, Heinrich Albertz, who was a Protestant pastor by profession. Those who went into the business of organising escapes can be divided into two categories: those who provided an honest and efficient service for a fee and those who took money and frequently failed to deliver the goods. In between, as is usually the case, there was a grey area. The sordid world of organised crime moved into trafficking in human beings on a large scale and syndicates were formed to exploit the possibilities. Blackmail, extortion and physical violence soon began to develop, and even murder. Gangs betrayed their rivals to the State Security Service and even burgled each others' premises to steal lists of contacts and useful forged documents. One could go so far as to describe these elements as a form of industry with its elite of managers and, below them, the skilled workmen – the couriers, the forgers and the mechanics who welded secret compartments into cars.

The West Berlin police even set up a special department to deal with the criminal side of the escape industry, but frequently found their hands tied. Witnesses were difficult to find or if found were threatened, and evidence was more often than not unreliable. A further problem was the fact that they could not co-operate in any way with their opposite numbers on the other side of the Wall, who themselves were waging their own war on the criminals from a different point of view. Berlin was riddled with informers and agents even in police headquarters, who would leak information about investigations to either side, either for a price or from political motives. On top of all this, there was the involvement of the Allied secret services, all of whom have a considerable presence in West Berlin. They availed themselves of the services of the well-organised syndicates for bringing out people in whom they were interested.

One man who was particularly involved with the CIA was Dietrich Jensch, a huge squarely-built extrovert who was a well-known figure around the less respectable bars and nightclubs in West Berlin. His wife ran the Empress Bar. Jensch teamed up with two men, Albert Schutz who was also a bar owner, and Karl-Heinz Bley who had once been a butcher. Their organisation was always reckoned to be the most reliable in terms of success and their profits were enormous. Jensch and his partners worked on the basis of payment for success, lost few of their clients and brought out several hundreds over the years. Their activities were always nebulous and those who were helped on behalf of the Americans had anyway to sign a declaration of secrecy. Others stayed silent to protect relatives who remained in the East or so as not to betray the actual method used to the DDR secret police. Co-operation with Allied secret service organisations always hampered the West Berlin police, who under the occupation status were required to take orders from them. The CIA even armed Jensch, who was reputed to carry a rifle behind the dashboard of his Chevrolet Impala.

Jensch and Schutz, before Bley joined them, were credited with having brought out nearly four hundred refugees by the end of 1964, using forged passports. Few countries in the West had ever recognised the DDR and the authorities there were very keen to enter the club of respectable nations and to be taken seriously. In addition, the authorities had to swallow the diplomatic disaster of having built the Wall and the negative publicity that that entailed. Jensch and Schutz, who seemed to have an astute sense of psychology, utilised this need for recognition in their use of false diplomatic passports, knowing that DDR officials were unlikely to risk further opprobrium by questioning diplomatic travellers too closely. The two men had a whole series of 'diplomatic passports' manufactured in Spain, Greece and Turkey, which were simply products of pure fantasy. Each was enclosed in an opulent leather cover embossed in gold, with parchment pages inside covered with fancy stamps and copperplate writing. The frontier police never even noticed glaring spelling mistakes. The deception was aided by the rash of new third world states which were springing up at the time like mushrooms.

The idea had originated in the Bavarian Alps where Jensch had taken a winter sports holiday. He met a small-time swindler from Munich who had dreamed up a lucrative market in human snobbery which appealed to the status seekers and nouveau riche in West Germany. He founded what he called a CD club which provided members with diplomatic passports, CD plates and other such items. Jensch bought such a kit, seeing the possibilities, and with his new passport he succeeded in travelling back to Berlin by road through East Germany, without being detected. Soon they were making their own forgeries and even ran a fleet of large impressive American cars in which the refugee 'diplomats' travelled. The next idea from the Munich swindler was to manufacture United Nations passports which identified the bearer as an official of one of the many international organisations with extra-territorial status. Jensch and Schutz bought a selection of these and managed to smuggle more than a hundred clients into the West, in cars equipped with UNO plates on the front.

The swindler had assumed that Jensch was pulling the same trick as he was, selling the papers to status seekers, but when he found out the real reason he promptly upped the price. But by then, Jensch and Schutz had familiarised themselves with the passports and felt confident enough to manufacture their own, choosing a printer in Spain. The swindler, who found himself sitting on a load of passports, then decided to go into the escape business himself, but was lacking in the skill and experience of the real professionals. One of his cars with a driver and four refugees on board was stopped at the border and the East German police discovered the scheme which had been running so smoothly for months. They naturally complained to the United Nations about misuse of its official documents, only to be told that the organisation did not issue such papers. Yet the odd thing is that the deception continued unabated. Schutz and Jensch returned from Spain with their new stock which they continued to use until November 1964, when the scheme was finally betrayed.

Jensch retired in 1965, but Schutz could not resist the excitement and the money to be made from the refugee business. He carried on with Karl-Heinz Bley until well into the 1970s. It was they who dreamed up the idea of the hollow cable drum mounted on the back of a lorry. It could be entered via a flap in the side and on two occasions, four refugees were hidden inside and driven to safety. It seemed to be a foolproof method, but was discovered through betrayal. On the second run, one of the passengers was a 17-year-old girl who had left her parents behind in the East. When she arrived in West Berlin she was contacted by agents of the State Security Service. She was threatened that if she did not return voluntarily, her parents would be punished and that her father would have to suffer professional disqualification. All she had to do was to go home and own up to what she had done. She would not be punished and her parents would be left in peace. Subjected to such pressure, she went back and told the authorities all she knew.

Another of Bley's ideas was the famous trick with the stuffed cow, a Berlin variant of the Trojan Horse legend. He discovered the stuffed cow at the premises of a well-known taxidermist and by claiming that he needed it as a prop for a theatrical production, purchased it. The next step was to remove the stuffing from the belly and fit inside a reinforced compartment big enough to hide a slimly built person. Bley then applied for the necessary transit papers to ship it by road to West Germany where it was supposedly to appear on stage. Loaded on the back of a van, the cow was driven out of West Berlin on to the transit autobahn in the direction of the West German frontier at Helmstedt, but on the way the van made a brief stop in a lay-by, where a young woman jumped on board. Shortly before the checkpoint she climbed inside the cow and was passed through without suspicion. After a pause in West Germany for the duration of the supposed performance, the cow made its way back again to West Berlin, and again a refugee was picked up and safely delivered. It was the third trip that was unlucky, on a journey into Berlin. With a certain Monika Schubert on board, the van was stopped at the Drewitz checkpoint in July 1969. A suspicious frontier guard ordered the driver to open the crate and then the cow itself, finding the refugee cramped up inside. Both she and the driver were arrested, leaving her sorrowful boyfriend who had paid Bley for the trip.

Bley was particularly fond of the possibilities offered by the transit autobahns. There are three main road routes out of Berlin, one leading north-west to Hamburg, one to the east towards Hannover and a southern route into Bavaria via Hof. These are naturally well patrolled by the East German police who gain a substantial foreign exchange income for the state by persecuting motorists for minor infringements of their traffic laws. Motorists in transit are only permitted to stop in certain designated lay-bys and at special petrol stations and restaurants which take foreign currency, but the police cannot be everywhere. Many escapes have involved a quick stop at a lay-by to take on refugees and hide them in vehicles. It was Bley who thought up the idea of the egg lorry, which was a large box truck engaged in regular runs to and from Berlin with a cargo of eggs. Naturally, lorries in transit are sealed by the customs and on leaving the DDR these seals are examined most carefully for signs of tampering. On Bley's truck, however, there was a large egg shape on the side designed as a trade mark and this was made to swing open. At a designated place on the transit route the refugees would be waiting. A quick stop, in they would scramble and the egg symbol was refastened. At the border the sealed rear door would be intact and no undue suspicion would be aroused.

But even Schutz and Bley could fall victim to the greed and jealousy of others in the business. The two men were always casting around for new ideas and after the diplomatic trick could no longer be used, realised that there was another privileged elite in West Berlin – Allied servicemen in uniform. Under the four-power occupation status of the divided city, members of the Russian, British, French and American armed forces can freely move in each other's sectors without being required to show anything more than their identity cards. This right of passage is scrupulously adhered to by both sides, who send daily 'flag tours' through the city. Every morning you can see a staff car with four Russian officers in it drive through Checkpoint Charlie for a tour of West Berlin. The Western Allies do the same in the East. It may well be that the two men got the idea from a successful escape that made headlines in the West Berlin newspapers in early 1965. Four young East Berliners managed to get hold of a Russian limousine of the type used by the army and painted it matt khaki. The girlfriend of one of them was a tailoress by trade, and she manufactured four extremely passable Russian uniforms, complete with the correct insignia of rank. When all was ready, they hid the girl in the car and coolly drove through Checkpoint Charlie, haughtily returning the salutes of the frontier guards. At any rate, Schutz and Bley got hold of two genuine American uniforms and identity cards by purchasing them from impecunious GIs. Dressing themselves in the uniforms, the two partners made a dummy run by walking around in West Berlin without being challenged. It is even said that Schutz's sergeant's stripes were sewn on the wrong way up.

At the time (1965), the American army used German Ford Taunus cars and such a vehicle was easy enough to obtain and to respray in the correct (drab) olive colour. The necessary number plates were also obtained. The plan was for a driver to take the car on its West German plates into East Berlin, with the American plates hidden under the seat and the two uniforms concealed inside the spare tyre. There he would rendezvous with a couple in their twenties and the switch would be made. The driver and the man would put on the uniforms and the girl would be hidden in a secret compartment. Then they would simply drive back through the checkpoint as if they were returning from a 'flag tour'.

The driver was to be a certain Horst Schramm, a West German merchant seaman who spoke quite good English with a strong American accent, and he was to be paid a fee. What then transpired was later to be revealed in court, and is an interesting insight into the morals and activities of the professional escape organisers. Schramm was approached by a rival group who offered him money to reveal the whole operation to them. Either for moral reasons or because he was scared of what Schutz and Bley might do to him, he declined but, in a spirit of free enterprise, decided to make a bit on the side. Schramm agreed with the rival firm to bring out an extra refugee, one of their 'customers' in return for an extra fee – a fact which he did not reveal to his original paymasters.

The actual trip was executed on 19 December 1965. Schramm, as a West German, drove into East Berlin via the Heinrich Heinestrasse checkpoint and made his way to the first rendezvous, where he picked up the refugee for the rival syndicate, who was a doctor's wife. Then he picked up the other two as part of the original plan. After he had hidden the car in some woods, the doctor's wife was concealed in the boot. Then he and the young man put on the American uniforms, changed the number plates and stuck the Stars and Stripes flag on the bonnet. The other woman was hidden away under the dashboard. The return journey was simplicity itself. The two GIs passed through Checkpoint Charlie on the Eastern side without let or hindrance, and when they came to the American border post, they simply drove past at speed and disappeared into the traffic. A successful escape and a method which could probably have been used time and time again.

But somehow a week later a newspaper in Germany which specialises in sensational reporting got hold of the story and even printed a photograph of Schramm posing as an American sergeant. It is probable that he sold the story in order to improve his earnings from the trip. Naturally this alerted the authorities who arrested Schutz, Bley and Schramm and started a major investigation. The two Americans who had parted with their uniforms and identity papers were court-martialled by their own authorities. The three Germans were charged with a number of offences including impersonation, forgery and theft, and were duly sentenced to terms of imprisonment. During the trial, Schutz openly boasted that he had already made over a million marks from his activities, and was highly annoyed at being found guilty. The three promptly appealed and called a press conference, at which they alleged that their activities had been tacitly supported by various official bodies including the West Berlin Senate, and that they had been promised protection if arrested. They went on to claim that their organisation served the public good and that they were being pilloried because of political pressure.

Because of regular publicity, the identities of some of the organisers were well known, although in those early years they tended not to advertise. Generally, the services of a middle man or broker were employed to put a customer in touch with a suitable firm, for which he received a commission. A former medical student by the name of Strobel operated from an apartment in West Berlin and made a small fortune by matching suitable business partners.

One of the most unpleasant specimens who emerged from the dimly lit world of clip joints and seedy bars was a former taxi driver by the name of Kurt Wordel, nicknamed 'The Shark' by his detractors. Before the West Berlin police were finally able to nail him, he had made a fortune and left a trail of despair and misery in his wake. Jensch, Schutz and Bley carried out well-planned and successful escapes for their money, but Wordel's work was slipshod and incompetent. Although he claimed to have helped some three hundred and fifty refugees, at least a hundred ended up in Communist prisons and countless others were milked of their money. Typical of one of his operations was one in which an innocent party suffered and in which Wordel himself took no part, being content to remain in the background. He had been commissioned to bring over an East German girl aged 22, and charged two accomplices with the mission, Klaus Lindner and Joachim Podelski. What was needed was a dupe with West German citizenship, who was found in the person of an 18-year-old from Hildesheim, Gisela Boldorf. She firstly resembled the refugee, Angelika Probst, and secondly had been in trouble with the police in the past for suspected prostitution. She was persuaded by Lindner to take part in the classic substitution ploy for a promised fee. They would both go over to East Berlin on day visas and her papers would be handed over to the refugee. All Gisela had to do was to go to the authorities and complain that her papers had been stolen, and she would then be allowed back over the border. They drove over in Lindner's car, and in a cafe he took her coat and West German passport, returning to the West with the refugee, leaving Gisela stranded. She, believing Lindner's tales, simply went off to the police and claimed that she had been robbed, but was not believed. She was tried and sentenced to eighteen months in prison for being an accomplice, although she served only five months before being released.

For this particular effort, Wordel and his two companions provided enough evidence for the West German police to frame a case. The three men were arrested and Lindner confessed his part in the deception. Wordel got eighteen months and the two other men twelve months apiece. In the police files, however, there was a whole string of sordid deceptions that could be laid at the door of Wordel and his associates. A young West German asked Wordel to bring out his girlfriend Brigitte Ebner and paid him 8000 DM. Wordel decided to use a plan which was tried and trusted and had already worked several times in the past. Brigitte and another girl were to be secreted in a car with false Monaco plates and driven from Czechoslovakia into Austria, by an American named Robert Kalakau who was married to a German and lived in Bavaria. Seemingly unknown to Kalakau, Wordel, from motives either of vanity or greed, sold the story of how they had been outwitting the Czechs to two freelance journalists who themselves, naturally enough, sold the material on, complete with photographs, to among other sources, *Life* magazine. If he had known, Kalakau would hardly have been stupid enough to try to pull the same stunt yet again. Inevitably he was caught on the border and sentenced to twelve months in prison, while the two girls were deported back to East Germany. Wordel was not particularly worried as he had pocketed the fee in advance, but Brigitte's boyfriend, having not heard anything more, decided to investigate. He went off to East Berlin and knocked at her door, which was opened by a State Security Service man who promptly arrested him as being an accomplice. The unfortunate young man not only lost his money, but spent several months in prison and never saw the girl again.

Wordel's greed prompted him to cut corners with criminal

99

disregard for the human consequences. It was even said that when he discovered that one particular refugee was pregnant, he charged an extra half-fee for the unborn child. One day he was approached by an elderly lady who lived in West Berlin, who asked him to smuggle out her daughter, son-in-law and the couple's 4-year-old child. In return for his help she parted with her life savings of some 10,000 marks. The young family were contacted by a courier at their flat in Leipzig and were told to go to East Berlin and there to wait for further word. Apparently they waited for several weeks in a dingy boarding house before their false papers arrived, which showed them to be an Italian family who had been on holiday. They then duly boarded the train but when they presented their papers were promptly arrested and taken off the train. The date was missing from one visa and other official passport stamps had been put in the wrong place. The arrest had been witnessed by the courier who reported back to Wordel, but he did not have the decency to inform the mother. He kept telling her to be patient and even gave her false dates when her family would arrive. The couple were of course imprisoned, but in 1966 they were permitted to leave and settle in the West.

Mention has been made earlier of the idealist Harry Seidel and of how he became involved on the fringe with the professionals. One of those with whom he associated was Fritz Wagner, known as 'the fat one'. In order to create an aura of respectability, he made use of young students as a front. Behind the scenes, however, his associates were mainly recruited from the ranks of the lesser underworld. One of his keenest rivals was a certain Uwe Hass who had at one time been closely involved with Kurt Wordel. In the autumn of 1965, Hass was engaged to bring a young couple out of East Berlin, and decided to use a car of which several escape organisers were fond, the Citröen ID or DS 19. These bulky cars have plenty of empty space within their contours, of which the favourite was the hollow area inside the front wings, large enough to secrete a person on each side. The author has been told on good authority of another ploy used with the same sort of car. Inevitably the DDR specialists began to use heat-seeking equipment to try to trace the body warmth of refugees in secret compartments. As an answer to this, someone came up with the idea of hollowing out the plump upholstery of the Citröen driver's seat. Once inserted inside the shell of the seat, a small refugee could be placed in a sitting position, with the actual driver sitting virtually on his or her lap. When the driver had to get out during a vehicle search, the guards would assume that heat from the seat emanated from the residual warmth of the driver.

But to return to the saga of Hass and Wagner. The Citröen conversion was carried out by a specialist mechanic in a back-alley workshop, who was well known in the trade. Through the grapevine, Wagner heard of the idea and commissioned a similar car from the same workshop. On the day of the escape, Hass had prepared everything meticulously, but oddly enough his car suffered a breakdown on the way to the border – due to a quantity of sugar in the petrol tank as was subsequently discovered. Wagner then appeared and offered to take over the run, which he completed successfully. The final twist came, however, when Hass discovered that the two refugees who were thus brought out had been spying for the Wagner organisation, and after their escape, went to work for him. Now as fate would have it, the two were arrested shortly afterwards in East Berlin where they had acted as couriers, equipped with false papers and Wagner's Citröen. Naturally enough, Hass denied having tipped off the State Security Service, but revenge is sweet and there is little honour among such figures. Wagner too was finally brought to trial and imprisoned during a massive crackdown by the West Berlin police.

Since the late 1960s, escapes have tended to take place away from Berlin, as the West German police have applied more pressure and East German anti-escape methods have become increasingly sophisticated. Once the whole gamut of false passports, diplomatic papers and cars with hidden compartments had been worked through, the hard core of Berlin professionals faded into the background. Those who remained in the business became far more discreet, while many others retired to enjoy the profits. We have seen that Wolfgang Fuchs shifted his activities to moving refugees out through other Eastern bloc countries and this is now the accepted method. Syndicates and organisations grew up in West Germany, mainly centred in Munich, which operated for considerable fees, and foreigners also got in on the act. Hans Lenzlinger, a Swiss citizen based in Zurich, even advertised his services in the newspapers and in his early days was not averse to publicity, which all helped to boost his reputation. He seems to have started work in 1971, as a side-line to his export-import business, and was still going strong in the early 1980s.

It was the publicity surrounding the escape of a woman in her thirties, crippled by polio, that led to the discovery of Lenzlinger. Ellen Rieske travelled by train to Prague and then on to a prearranged rendezvous in the forest area near to the border. There she was picked up and secreted in a secret compartment in a large American car, behind which was a horsebox. This contained a racehorse which had been bought in Czechoslovakia, and when they arrived at the border with East Germany, the Czech guards gave only a casual glance at the car, before swarming all over the horsebox. Meanwhile, inside the compartment, the lady was suffering both from lack of ventilation and from the fact that three pet tortoises that she had insisted on bringing with her were crawling all over her body. Her escape was successful and she was reunited with her fiancé in Switzerland, but the horse ended up in a West German pet food factory, as Lenzlinger had failed to obtain the necessary import certificate for Switzerland.

The next chapter deals in detail with the career of a notable modern escape organiser who was to become notorious at the time of the 25th anniversary celebrations, but there are others. If you visit some of the observation platforms which the West Berlin authorities have erected to enable visitors to look over the Wall, you will probably see small adhesive labels attached to the handrails. The message on them is addressed to 'those who may be experiencing difficulty in transferring their place of residence from the DDR to West Germany or West Berlin!' Those involved are requested to telephone a West Berlin number, which is an initial contact for advice about the problem and is a cover for an escape organiser.

Ironically Wolfgang Fuchs stated in a recent interview that, in his opinion, one could well start building tunnels again with a good chance of success, for the simple reason that a whole generation of police had grown up on the other side of the Wall who would have no memory of the heady days of the early 1960s.

8

Wolf Quasner

Wolf Quasner is 47 years old and describes himself as an antique dealer at times, and at other times as a clairvoyant. He also has business cards which state that he is the director of 'The Escape Planning Bureau'. Much of his background and subsequent activities are of necessity nebulous and he is known to the East German authorities as an escape organiser. What follows is based on a series of interviews he gave the author who, in spite of recent press publicity, is prepared to give him the credit for altruism. His story and some of the escapes which he planned are quite remarkable.

In his late teens he worked for an organisation in West Berlin which printed a magazine called *Tarantula*. This was a blatant anti-Communist propaganda magazine financed by American sources such as Radio Liberty and the CIA. These magazines were smuggled into the East by travellers and were distributed over the frontier by balloon. On Sunday 13 August 1961, Wolf was in the Eastern sector visiting his girlfriend and during the morning they switched on the radio, only to hear that the Wall was being built. Naturally his girlfriend pleaded with him to take her back with him, since he assumed that as a West Berliner he would be allowed to leave. While she was packing a few things another girl came round to the flat and saw the preparations for departure. She wanted to go as well, so Wolf bundled the two of them into the boot of his car. Luckily for them, the police were mainly engaged in Wall building and anyway there were hordes of West Berliners trapped on the wrong side of the Wall. He was able to drive through without difficulty and took the two girls to his grandmother's flat. There, they took some sheets from the cupboard and painted slogans on them, before joining the mass demonstration at the Brandenburg Gate. His grandmother was not amused at the loss of her bedding in the cause of German unity, but Wolf himself was immortalised in a press photograph.

During the early 1960s, Wolf was a small part of the escape scene. The skills he had learnt working for the propaganda magazine were turned to good use when he became an accomplished forger. We have already mentioned that to discourage the simple substitution of photographs in West German identity cards, the East Germans resorted to the use of currency exchange certificates with a duplicate that had to be lodged at the point of entry. Wolf specialised in levering off photographs and pasting in others, and then went into the faking of passport stamps. The method of getting around the foreign exchange certificate problem was as follows. False ones were printed, filled out in the West and correctly stamped. A full set of papers including a West German identity card would be smuggled into East Berlin by a courier and given to the refugee, together with a train ticket to an official exit point on the Baltic. The refugee was ostensibly in transit through East Berlin, and would not exit through his point of entry so that it was impossible to compare the exchange certificate duplicate. This worked well for a while, until an astute official noticed that he had collected more certificates than the East Berlin checkpoint had issued. The result was that at entry, each certificate was given a random number which was then telexed to the control point at the traveller's point of departure from the DDR.

The next step in the forgery was the introduction of printed entry visa forms for West Germans and foreigners entering East Berlin. The colour and design of these was changed each day to deter clandestine manufacture, but Wolf and others who were in the same line of business were not defeated for long. Two couriers would cross over early in the morning, and while one stayed behind, the other would return with his example of the permit of the day. On arrival in the West, this would be examined for signature, stamp, serial number and colour, and a copy would be made. This would be taken back to the East, together with a false West German identity card, by a third courier. His job was to pass the forgeries on to the refugee and give his own permit back to the original courier, who meanwhile had probably been sitting in a pub.

Wolf made an unspectacular living out of his talents for forgery, but was not prepared to take the existence of the Wall lying down. Still involved in radical politics on the right wing, he attempted to blow it up. Based on knowledge gained during chemistry lessons at school, he and a few friends made a bomb which they placed one night against the Wall, then lit the fuse and ran. Just as the 3-minute fuse began to burn, along came two policemen who saw the bomb and also decided to take cover – in exactly the same place where Wolf and his companions had hidden. Together they watched the explosion which blew a considerable hole in the concrete slabs. Then the two officers walked off in a different direction. The explosion was not planned as part of an escape, but purely as a demonstration against the inhumanity of walling-in the city. It was a gesture that received maximum publicity, especially the subsequent photograph of two East German officers looking ruefully at the damage.

In the late 1970s, Wolf went into business on his own account, together with an older man who is still his partner today. Wolf had seen the advent of the criminals and of the misery they caused, and he set out to provide an honest service for a reasonable fee, smuggling his refugees out via other Eastern bloc countries. Forgery was to remain his speciality but with a high degree of flair and imagination. When he recounts some of his escapades, one has to admire his cheek. One of his early coups was carried out at the time of the Pope's first visit to Poland in 1979. The Holy Father and his immediate entourage naturally travelled by air, but the horde of camp followers which are necessary for such an overseas trip were transported from Italy by train. When they left, the retinue had grown and included three extra priests and two extra nuns – all East Germans and all in correct clerical garb. The Polish authorities were so much on their best behaviour at the time that it was not a case of 'we counted them all in and we counted them all out again'.

Essentially the system that Wolf Quasner developed and used scores of times relied on forged diplomatic passports, a new variant of the old trick. He set up a complete organisation to copy and reproduce genuine passports, and to manufacture the necessary stamps, visas and other papers. As an example of his cheek, he even concocted a passport from a country that did not exist except in his imagination. It is perfect, complete inside with a signed declaration from the 'President of the Peoples' Revolutionary Council' and an impressive gold embossed coat of arms on the front. This, together with many others, examples of rubber stamps, false number plates and photographs are displayed in cabinets on the wall of a bar called 'The Oasis', in a small street in West Berlin. The proprietor is an Austrian, Dieter Bergner, who when he took it over, wanted to call it 'The Escape Helper', an idea which was turned down by the licensing authorities.

Dieter worked for many years for Wolf as a courier, a vital link in the organisation of any escape, and started in 1970. As an Austrian and citizen of a neutral country, it was far easier for him to move about through Eastern bloc borders, often without the need for a visa. It was a life of fear and loneliness, from which he has since retired with honour after his cover was blown. He says that the only Eastern countries that he can still visit are Hungary and Yugoslavia, elsewhere he is persona non grata. His relationship with Wolf was based on mutual trust without which they would have been unable to operate as a team. He described Wolf as the brains and himself as the executant.

When Wolf received a commission and accepted it, the first step was to check out, as far as was humanly possible, the people involved. He would naturally receive their passport photographs and would know where they lived. He might show them around the refugee community and ask: 'Is this Dr so and so?' Another method was to compare their names and addresses with the corresponding East German telephone directories, or he would send a courier to their home town to make discreet enquiries. Only then would they be contacted personally and be given their orders, usually to travel to Warsaw, Prague or Budapest and to stay at a certain hotel. Passwords and identity checks would also be established. Dieter described a typical escape by train.

At the beginning you make contact with the people who are to travel, you hand over their papers and tell them what they have to do. I would always say to them that these are diplomatic papers, so you must act like diplomats. Walk proudly, don't grovel. Then I would see to it that they got to the station and safely on to the train. I always sat one coach away from them so that by looking out of the window I could see if anything had happened to them. Once they were through the last control before the West German border, I had to go to them and take away their false papers, which I then had to quickly destroy in the toilet as they were not permitted to show them in Germany. Besides, I didn't want them to be in the position to say that I was the man who had given them the forgeries. Then I would have been for the high jump as well.

The reason for this was that in 1980 the West German government made it illegal to forge even foreign documents, which made life awkward for the escape helpers who had tended to rely on such deceptions. It is not a crime to help someone to escape, but it is to supply them with forged identity documents. Dieter became such a regular on the run from Prague to Nuremberg that he was well known at the frontier station at Schirnding. He remembers that on one occasion he was sitting in the train when the West German customs and border police came into his compartment. One said to the other: 'Hey, Hans, Dieter is on the train, there must be some escapees somewhere.' Wolf was usually at Schirnding to meet the train which arrived at 4 o'clock in the morning.

I would take a taxi from the hotel to the station and when I got there, one of the border police would see me. Then he would go into the office because he would know that some-thing was going on. Soon there would be eight or ten police on the platform because they would know that there would be people from East Germany on the train.

On arrival in the West, the refugees would be given an initial questioning while the courier left with the train on which they had arrived. After about two hours the refugees would be able to leave and Wolf would then take them on the next train. He described the scene early in the morning standing on the deserted platform just before dawn and watching the hands of the station clock. Then he would hear the noise of the train and see the headlamps coming around the curve of the track from the Czech border point. He would be looking out for the courier who would give him a sign that everything was OK. 'Then I knew that the family would be in the next coach. Walking along the platform, I don't know exactly where they are. But I see four persons in a compartment and I know the faces from the photographs.' Later, when they had been released by the authorities and were in the next train, he would go up to them and say: 'My name is Wolf. Welcome to the West.'

Behind such an apparently simple procedure, however, there was a high degree of technical expertise involved, in order to outwit the various Eastern bloc authorities. Everything was precisely planned on military lines. It was not enough simply to sit in a bar in West Berlin and dream up a good idea. Wolf's expertise in forgery went beyond manufacturing passports, and into such fields as ink analysis and chromatography. This became necessary when the East Germans started to use inks which change colour under ultraviolet light. What looks like an ordinary passport stamp takes on a completely different dimension, and some of the more complicated stamps are printed in different colours, that could be changed at random, sometimes daily. Wolf has a miniature laboratory complete with a high-powered microscope, racks of coloured inks, printers' colour charts and an ultraviolet lamp. The worst problem, though, was the practice of introducing number codes on to rubber stamps, which again were changed at random. This necessitated an early run by a courier to obtain a sample of the stamp of the day, as described earlier, but what if there was insufficient time to transfer a competent forgery on to the false passports to be used by the refugees? Wolf found the answer when he visited a photographic exhibition – a new type of film sensitive to infrared light of low intensity. Using this, he realised that a rubber stamp could be manufactured in the toilet compartment of a train. The system works like this.

The courier, taking his own passport and the forged ones, goes to the toilet equipped with his normal washing and shaving gear. The necessary chemicals are contained in innocent looking after-shave lotion bottles and shaving cream jars. The two halves of the soap dish double up as developing and fixing baths. He puts a piece of film on the genuine stamp, on top of which comes an elastoplast roll as distance piece, and then a torch with an infrared bulb. The film is then exposed for about six minutes and developed to give a negative. Under the negative a thick piece of sensitive paper is placed which is again exposed to the torch for a few minutes. When the paper is developed the light has the effect of burning out the background which can then be scraped away with a razor blade – leaving only the high spots which will make the necessary impression. This can then be inked on a pad and used as often as required, assuming that the ink has been analysed and the courier has a selection of the most likely colour combinations. Just in case any reader might be tempted to think that the author has imagined this, Wolf demonstrated the technique before the camera when 'Hanni Sends Her Love' was made, the operation being carried out in the confines of a caravan toilet as we could not obtain the use of a railway carriage. All the film crew who were watching were able to satisfy themselves that a workable rubber stamp image was created before their eyes under conditions similar to those that would be encountered on an operation.

Wolf is sometimes cynical about the motives of his customers and has many tales to tell. Such as the one about the wealthy West German businessman who went to East Berlin frequently on business. There he met an attractive girl who begged him to help her escape as she was in love with him and could not live without him, and so on. The man in question was not short of money and he engaged Wolf to manage the operation, which he did and for which he received his fee. On arrival, the girl was naturally sent to the reception centre for refugees near Giessen to be processed, where she met her boyfriend and went off with him – leaving the businessman both poorer and wiser. Another man paid to have his supposed girlfriend brought out, and when Wolf arrived at Frankfurt Airport with her, it transpired that the two hardly knew each other, which he found highly suspicious.

Both Wolf and Dieter have had some anxious moments over the years, one of which concerned the escape of a family of East Germans who were due to fly out from Warsaw on a Pan American aircraft. Dieter remembers very well what happened.

It was a family, father, mother and a child, identified as the Heuser family on forged Austrian passports. We were already through the controls and in the departure lounge when the flight was called. We were taken by bus out to the aircraft, found our seats and the engines were started. I was just about to breathe a sigh of relief when suddenly there was an announcement over the intercom – 'Will the Heuser family please report to the flight personnel'. I looked towards the front and there was this man from the passport control standing there. The engines were switched off again and 'Mr Heuser' went forward looking as white as a sheet. As he went by I managed to whisper to him not to get off the aircraft as it was extra-territorial and he could not be arrested on board. Well, he showed the passports to the official who then demanded over the pilot's radio that the control tower connect him to the first secretary of the Austrian Embassy. Then we waited until this gentleman could get out to the airport. The atmosphere on board was stifling, but then the diplomat arrived and was shown the passports. Well, he knew quite well that they were not real, but he certified that they were genuine. So, after at least an hour's delay we were permitted to take off. I asked the steward if it would be possible to speak to the captain. He asked me to come into the cockpit and I told him and I was sorry about the delay, which was my fault. I asked him not give the real reason over the radio to Frankfurt, our destination, as we might be overheard and forced down. I also apologised to the steward who said how pleased he was for all of us, and then served champagne all round. When we got to Frankfurt, ten police-men with bullet-proof vests and pistols came on board as they thought that there might have been a highjack or some-thing like that. But the steward said, 'no, no, these are only people fleeing from the DDR.'

In the meantime, Wolf had been pacing up and down at the airport, plagued by doubts. But then the arrival was announced and Dieter was one of the first to come through. He briefly acknowledged Wolf and then quickly disappeared into the crowd as he still had to dispose of the false passports. Wolf also spent anxious moments at exactly the same place on another occasion, waiting for the Warsaw flight, but that time Dieter did not come through. For Dieter, it was the end of his career as a courier.

The story started when Wolf had a visitor who told him that a doctor wished to escape from East Berlin with his family, and he agreed to take on the operation. A fee was agreed and the necessary photographs were delivered.

So we checked up. We sent a courier over with the pictures and he identified the man – he really was Doctor so and so. When I looked at the pictures I saw that the man was good looking, like a soldier. Jokingly I said that he looks like a major, so we gave him the code name Major X. All the people who worked on this job knew him as that.

When all the arrangements had been completed the family was told to go to Warsaw and stay at the Victoria Intercontinental Hotel. From then on it was all up to Dieter. He travelled to Warsaw and booked into the same hotel. After that he went down to the lounge and sat in an armchair reading the news-paper, his eyes roving around the whole area for any hint of danger. Everything seemed to be perfectly in order, so he turned his gaze on a family group sitting quietly on their own and watched them for a while, comparing their faces with the pictures in the false passports which he had ready to give them. Once again, there was no hint of danger, so he got up, went over to them and gave the password. The doctor looked up and made a gesture with his hand, upon which eight plain-clothes men appeared as if from nowhere and Dieter found himself handcuffed.

He was hustled out of the hotel and off to the headquarters of the Polish secret police where he was interrogated before being thrown into a cell. He had visions that it was going to mean a lengthy stay and probable transfer to East Germany to stand trial as an escape helper. But after a while he was taken in front of a captain who told him that he did not have to worry as they were not interested in handing him over to the DDR. The officer went on to say that as far as the Polish authorities were concerned, their ends were not served by Dieter sitting in a prison cell and that they would far rather extract a ransom in hard currency for him. If he could raise a substantial sum in bail, he could go home 'pending a decision on prosecution'.

In the meanwhile Wolf was at the airport. The flight had arrived on time and Dieter was not on board – nor were the 'refugees'. After a while he was called to the information desk, feeling very worried, to be told that there was a phone call for him. On the other end was Dieter's wife who was also worried, as it was his custom to contact her immediately on arrival. Wolf told her that flights were often overbooked or party officials claimed seats at the last minute. Probably her husband would be on the next aircraft due in a few hours time. So there was a further wait and when he still did not arrive, Wolf was certain that he had been arrested and had to telephone Dieter's wife and tell her of his fears. She met Wolf at Berlin Airport and they sat up all night in the hope that he might get a message through to them.

The following morning Wolf put a call through to the DDR, to the supposed doctor's office, where it was confirmed that he was at work that day. Therefore Wolf reasoned that he must have been working all along for the secret police, for otherwise the whole family would have been arrested for attempting to escape. The betrayal was carried out through internal rather than external circumstances, and they had all been deceived. There was, however, no news of Dieter and Wolf assumed the worst, when to his surprise the following day he received a call from the Polish consulate. They told him that Dieter had been

28. *Ilse and Philip Hewitt relive old memories in 1986.*

29. *Wolfgang Fuchs – heroic tunnel builder.*

30. *Wolf Quasner and Peter Meyer in 1986.*

Mit Maschinenpistolen, Stacheldraht und Panzerwagen halten sie das Volk in Schach. Schwerbewaffnete Soldaten der sogenannten Volksarmee bewachen gemeinsam mit der „Volkspolizei" die Straßensperren an der Sektorengrenze in Berlin. Brutale Gewalt ist das letzte Mittel der SED, um die Flucht von Millionen Menschen aus dem „ersten Arbeiter- und Bauernstaat auf deutschem Boden" zu unterbinden. An der verbarrikadierten Sektorengrenze, die Ulbricht mit Rückendeckung der Sowjetunion und ihrer übrigen Satelliten zur Staatsgrenze erklärt hat, protestierte die West-Berliner Bevölkerung gegen die Willkürmaßnahmen (Bild unten: Am Brandenburger Tor). Sie tat dies auch stellvertretend für die Ost-Berliner und die Mitteldeutschen, die noch vom 7. Juni 1953 her wissen, wie der Bolschewismus jede freie Meinungsäußerung unterdrückt.

Deutsche Zeitung   Fotos: Berlin-Bild/dpa

31. *Wolf Quasner as a young man.*

32. *The extraordinary transformation of Peter Meyer.*

33. *Hanni safe in Berlin.*

arrested but would be released if the sum of 15,000 dollars could be lodged as security for his return to face eventual charges. Wolf raised the money and handed over the draft, in return for which Dieter was put on an aircraft and allowed to fly out to freedom. To this day he has never received a summons or any further communication from the Polish government. But the affair did mean that his career was at an end, although he is still involved in planning operations, where his intimate knowledge of foreign airports is of great value.

Wolf Quasner is scathing about escape organisers who fail to carry out their promises and who are criminals, but he is not concerned about the genuine ones.

I don't care if they have houses in Spain and money in the bank. If they help the refugees, then it is OK. But most of them are rogues. There is one type who says that he is an escape helper and demands his fee in advance. Then he says to the family you have to go to such and such a place and wait, and then we will come and collect you. But they don't turn up. They just pocket the money and it gets spent in the nightclubs and on gambling. Then there are others who also demand money in advance, but they make an effort to get the people out – a bit of one anyway. They buy an old rusty car for about 500 marks. It just has to be big enough to get the people in the boot. Then they go around the railway stations and look for a down and out who's an alcoholic or on drugs. They ask him if he has a driving licence and if he says yes, they offer him a few hundred marks to do a quick job. He is told to take the car along the Autobahn to West Germany and to stop at a certain kilometre sign. There some people will be waiting, so he must open the boot and let them get in. Most of the time they all get arrested at the border and sit for a long time in prison. But the escape helper doesn't care because out of the advance he has only forked out for the car and what he paid the driver.

On at least two occasions, Wolf has had to mount a rescue operation for refugees who have been left stranded and penniless by the criminal end of the business. On the first occasion,

Herr and Frau Riego moved from East Berlin to West Berlin, having reached pensionable age. They had sold their small house and their car, and had 55,000 marks in cash. Their aim was to invest this in getting their children out to join them. They made enquiries and found an escape helper willing to take on the job but who demanded all their cash in advance. Their son, their daughter and her husband and their child went into hiding in another East European country to wait for the courier, who never came. The elderly couple heard nothing and when they tried to find the helper, he had disappeared from the scene, naturally with their money, and it was several more weeks before they were put in touch with Wolf Quasner. He agreed to bring out the family, and after crossing several frontiers they arrived safely in West Berlin. His fee was waived until they had been able to get jobs and could afford to repay him.

A similar case resulted in Wolf pulling what must surely have been his most spectacular stunt to date, in the spring of 1984. Peter Meyer lived with his wife Hanni and their 4-year-old son, Markus, in East Berlin. Peter worked as a track repairer for the state railway system, and every day he saw the inter-zonal trains moving along with the signs on the coaches to such places as London, Amsterdam, Paris and Milan. Places which an East German can only dream about. He looked in through the windows and saw people sitting inside possessing the freedom to travel wherever they wanted to, and steadily his desire to escape increased until it became an obsession. His wife too was discontented with their primitive living conditions. Every evening she watched Western television and dreamed of a fur coat and a large car. Peter's mother had a friend who, because he was a pensioner, could visit West Berlin, and he was asked to try to find someone who would be prepared to get the family out. The man duly crossed the border one day and went to one of the seedier areas of West Berlin which is full of strip joints, bars and grubby clubs. There he had a drink or two, and plucking up courage, got into conversation with an Arab, who apparently had a mouth full of gold teeth and was dripping with expensive jewellery. The man explained the position and the Arab said yes, he was a

116

powerful escape organiser with all the necessary contacts. He would do the job for 20,000 marks in advance and could guarantee success. The Arab treated the East German pensioner to a meal in a restaurant, bought him drinks and sent him on his way to get the money. Back in the East he reported to the family that he had found the right man for the job.

With the help of his mother, Peter managed to scrape together the necessary funds, and once again the pensioner crossed the border, in somewhat of a panic in case he was searched. If he had been found with such a sum of Western currency on him, he would have spent a long time behind bars. Then he contacted the Arab, paid over the money and was told that the family would have to get everything ready and in two months time go to Prague. There they would be contacted and brought out. It all seemed so simple as Peter and Hanni disposed of most of their goods during their remaining few weeks, before booking train tickets to Prague, ostensibly for a holiday. Peter had no idea as to the method of their escape. He had simply been told that the family should go to the Wentzel Square in Prague at 8 o'clock in the evening on a certain date and stand by the statue. The square is only a few minutes walk from the railway station and they were early at the rendezvous point anyway. So they stood around and admired the scene on a fine spring evening, tense but optimistic. The time moved slowly on until 8 o'clock came and went, and no sign of their contact. They waited for a whole hour and then gave up.

Peter takes up the story. 'At first we were terribly disppointed. We didn't know what to do then and we certainly couldn't go back. So we decided to find a hotel and think over what could be done. We looked around and found the Hotel Flora where we were able to get a room.' Upstairs they sat and went over all the possibilities. 'We were there, we wanted to escape and would have to go on. We talked about the many tourists, the heavy-goods lorries, the possibility of getting in touch with someone.... One imagines all sorts of things, but then Markus had to be put to bed and by then it was quite late. I went down to the bar and had a few beers to calm my nerves.'

Sitting there on a bar stool, Peter noticed another man, who was obviously from the West, and they got into conversation.

It was that chance meeting in a foreign city that must surely have been directed by fate, a million to one throw of the dice.

We started to talk to each other over a few beers, and then I felt that I just had to get it all off my chest. So I told him everything. I don't know why, but I just had to talk to someone as I was totally down. I don't know why I chose him or whether I found him likeable. But when I had finished, he said, 'I'll help you'. He told me that we should stay at the hotel as it would take three or four days. Then he said that we would get a message from him, but first he would like to meet my family. I said that we could go up to the bedroom and by then I didn't care any more about what might happen. So we went upstairs and we told my wife. It was our last straw and we clung to it – it was all we had. He asked then if he could take some photographs of us all, so we got the little one out of bed. Then he said good-bye and left us on our own.

The man in the bar was a journalist, who felt sorry for the Meyer family and happened to know of Wolf Quasner's speciality. Wolf's telephone rang in West Berlin. 'This journalist called me and told me the story. A man, a woman and a small child stranded in Prague. He asked if I could help. I said yes, I could get the woman out and the child as we already had suitable papers for them, but the man would have to wait.'

In Prague the Meyers drummed their heels, prey to their fears and wondering what if anything would happen. In the afternoon of the following day they went to sit in the small lobby of the hotel and ordered something to drink. Then a stranger came to their table and asked if he could sit with them. Discreetly in the palm of his hand he held some photographs, the very same ones that had been taken the evening before in their bedroom.

He said that he was a courier from West Berlin, and could we talk in private. Well, I knew that the photos could only have come from the journalist who had actually taken them, so I reckoned that the man must be genuine. Even so, you still have to reckon with all sorts of things. So we went up to our room and he introduced himself with a single Christian name. Then he informed us of the situation. My wife and our son Markus would be taken out straight away, that same day. Naturally I asked about myself and he told me that they would arrange for me to escape but that it take a little while. First they had to find someone who looked like me. We all thought about it because at first we hesitated about the plan. We had come so far together and felt that it should be all or nobody. But then I said, go with him because on my own I might have an easier chance than the three of us. Even if I have to climb through somewhere, as alone I am more dextrous. The arguments went on for a bit but then we decided that we would do as the courier suggested. He repeated that it was one hundred per cent certain that they would come back for me. So, he took a photograph of my wife and then disappeared into the bathroom where he remained for about half an hour. When he emerged finally, he showed us a passport which had everything, even the picture of my wife all ready. It was difficult to say good-bye as one didn't really know what would happen, but anyway, the three of them left for the railway station while I stayed behind in the hotel.

Wolf met Hanni and Markus in West Berlin, and then turned his attention to the problem posed by the father. Peter is short, thick-set, with dark hair and a beard.

We looked around for a double, who had to be a foreigner of roughly the same age and build, without success. The situation was awful, with part of the family here in freedom and the father sitting and waiting. But then, after a few days we found a person who agreed to act as the double. The only problem was that he was a Ghanaian and extremely black. But then I thought, why not? The idea is a good one. So I started calling around to find a make-up artist from the theatre. I found several, but when I said that they would have to go to Czechoslovakia and make a white person into a black African, none of them was keen. They were all prepared to do it here in the West but not to go to a Communist country as it was too dangerous. Then eventually we

119

found a girl from Munich who was prepared to go. A further problem was that the family had no money to pay the expenses, and I had to send the make-up girl, the double, another coloured man to accompany Peter on his trip out and one of my own couriers to Prague. This was partly solved when the journalist who had made the original contact suggested that we make a video film of how Peter would escape to the West and then sell the story to the newspapers, to recoup some of the costs.

Wolf reasoned that there was always a danger in using a forged passport, and it was easier to falsify a face to fit the photograph in a genuine document than vice versa. He also reckoned that if the East German border guards saw a black man with a real passport with all the correct marks inside, they were hardly likely to suspect that he was one of their fellow citizens.

Peter in the meanwhile was feeling very lonely and out of touch, but after two days spent wandering around Prague, another of Wolf's couriers came up to him in the hotel. Without going into details, he showed Peter a photograph of his wife and son taken against an obviously Western background, and told him that everything had gone smoothly. He would just have to be patient for a little while longer.

After another four days I went down to breakfast at about 9 o'clock, sat down at a table and ordered some coffee. Nearby sat two black people which made me feel odd as they kept looking at me. I remember wondering if the secret police had started employing black people from Cuba. I felt really nervous as it seemed that they could look right through me. I wanted to get up and leave. Now my attention had concentrated on the two black men, one of whom had a beard just like mine, and I had not noticed a white couple sitting at the next table. I was just about to go, when the man came over to me and said, 'Hanni sends her love'. While I was recovering from the shock, he told me that the time had come and that we should go upstairs to my room. Once upstairs he said that I would be leaving Prague that day, and

I imagined that it would be just the same as had happened with my wife. But then he said that his female companion would first have to make a few alterations.

Peter did not know what to think and asked if he would have to lose his beard, only to be told that he would be able to keep it. So he stood there in the cheaply furnished room with this unknown couple who seemed to be waiting for something. Then there was a knock on the door and the two coloured men entered.

I thought that that was the end of the road. I would be arrested, but the courier told me to have a close look at the one with the beard. 'You will be made to look like that', he said. I just burst out laughing and said, 'That is impossible, that is unthinkable. Do you want to put some shoe polish on my face?' But then the woman opened a suitcase full of little bottles and tins and God knows what.

The transformation took several hours and was far more complicated than the application of some black cream. First Peter's hair was cut short and then curled with tongs and tissue paper so that it fitted close to his scalp just like the woolly thatch of an African. Then his nose was padded out to flare the nostrils and a black dye was applied, not only to his face but right down inside his neck and over his hands as well. This had to be capable of withstanding a lengthy journey without being affected by sweat or coming off if he should touch his face. The final touch was a pair of dark glasses to hide the unnatural whiteness of his eyes, and a smart suit, shirt and tie. When finished he looked every inch a pefect replica of a Ghanaian, and the whole transformation was captured on video tape.

But for Peter the next step was the worst moment of the whole operation, actually leaving the room.

It was terrible. I had been in that hotel for several days and all the staff knew me. I thought that they would all stare at me and wonder why I had smeared black stuff all over my face. But nothing happened. People just looked casually at

121

me. We went out into the corridor and my knees were knocking together, then down in the lift and through the crowded lobby. There was a car waiting outside and I was driven out to the airport together with the other coloured man who was to be my companion.

That other man was also a Ghanaian, who was there so as to answer any questions in English and he stuck beside Peter the whole way. The latter, having cleared the first hurdle of getting out of the hotel unrecognised, found his confidence growing, and even started to feel as if he really were black. At the airport they showed their papers and nobody took any notice of them at all, and it was the same story on arrival at the airport in East Berlin. From there they took the shuttle bus to the Friedrichstrasse station to catch the S-bahn into West Berlin. 'There we had to go down into a large hall where there was the first passport control. There they only looked at my papers and then we were through to the second control. There was a little hut where one had to push the passport through a window. The official banged in a stamp, the door opened and then we were allowed through on to the platform.' The wait for the train was only about five minutes, but to Peter it seemed like hours, and he felt that he had a white face. Only a few minutes away at the Zoo station, Wolf was waiting with Hanni and Markus, for a joyous reunion and freedom.

This type of operation with its attendant publicity has meant that Wolf Quasner has a fairly high profile in West Berlin although he states that he has not been personally molested by East German agents. He admits that his flat was raided by the West German police, looking for forged passports, and that he was fined heavily. His partner, who is an older man, had a very narrow escape, however, and the story is indicative of the thorough homework undertaken by the Ministry for State Security on the other side of the Wall. The partner is a gentleman of independent means and is fond of gambling – not for high stakes, but he enjoys the atmosphere of horse racing and casinos, as well as the company of ladies. One day not so long ago he was travelling in an aircraft and in the next seat was an attractive woman, with whom he got into conversation. During the course of the flight she told him that she was on her way back from Miami and that she had been having a flutter in the casinos in Nevada. Wolf's partner naturally pricked up his ears, and she went on to indicate that she owned a classy antique shop in Baden Baden, as well as a small stable of racehorses. He was well and truly hooked, and although married, was amenable to a discreetly managed affair. The two started seeing each other regularly at various social events around Europe, staying together in hotels and visiting jet set resorts. In Berlin, she was introduced to Wolf, who had dinner with them on several occasions at expensive restaurants. He was not suspicious but told her nothing about his activities – their conversation was restricted to antiques, about which she seemed well informed. Then one day she telephoned the partner and told him that she was in Prague and was having some small trouble with the authorities about her visa. Could he please come to Prague and give her some help? Quite naturally he was worried about the lady and made preparations to travel, but when Wolf heard about this, he advised strongly against going to Prague, scenting a trap. This is the type of ploy which John le Carré would call the 'honey trap'.

A few days later the lady in question appeared on East German television in an exposé of the activities of the escape-helping business. She described the partner exactly, including such details as what he drank and the make of cigarettes which he preferred. In the interview she also went into the methods they were using and the way in which passports were forged. For Wolf, who was furious, this was a clear illustration of the dangers of pillow talk.

The final twist to the Wolf Quasner story has to do with the period just before the 25th anniversary of the Wall in the summer of 1986, when his name and photograph appeared in newspapers all around the world. For a couple of days he became a local hero as a result of the spectacular escape of a refugee from East Berlin, disguised as a Russian soldier and in a car with three tailor's dummies dressed as officers. On the face of it, the official account was quite plausible. The refugee was a man by the name of Braun, who said that he had been helped by Quasner to escape in June. Originally he had been born in West Germany but had gone to live in the DDR during the late 1950s because of his political convictions. He soon became disillusioned, however, with the realities of life in a Communist state and as a result spent seven years in prison for a variety of offences including currency manipulation and persuading DDR citizens to leave and settle in the West. After he was released for the last time he ran a tyre repair workshop in East Berlin and lived with a divorcee. He had apparently agreed with her that when he escaped, she and her child would come out by the same route a few days later. When she failed to appear, Braun said that he persuaded Wolf to smuggle him back into East Germany so that he could find out what had gone wrong. Upon his return, he went to see his lady friend, who worked in the DDR Ministry of the Interior and she told him that she had decided to return to her ex-husband. Braun, as a result, was in grave difficulties and in hiding in East Berlin, so Quasner agreed to bring him out again, using a variant of another of the old tricks. Braun, as reported in all the papers, was the owner of a Russian Lada estate car of the type used by Soviet forces for their patrols in the Western sectors. He sprayed this up in the correct military colour and prepared the necessary false number plates. The rest of the props were smuggled in from West Berlin by one of Quasner's couriers. Wolf had noticed how stiffly the Russian soldiers always sat when driving through the checkpoints, never looking from side to side or showing any expression. He therefore supplied four Soviet army uniforms and three tailor's dummies of the type used to display clothes in shop windows.

At 7 o'clock in the evening of 30 July, the Lada estate car carrying the number CA 37–40 drove up to the Invalidenstrasse crossing point. The East German guards promptly raised the barrier and permitted the car to pass through, driven by a corporal who was carrying as passengers a lieutenant-colonel and two lieutenants. Once into the West, Braun drove the car, still dressed as a Russian, to the Kurfurstendamm, where he ordered a bottle of champagne at the 'Bristol'. Two days later, he gave a press conference on behalf of the *Arbeitsgemeinschaft 13 August*, the group which runs the museum at Checkpoint Charlie. In the presence of both Quasner and the director of the Museum, Dr Rainer Hildebrandt, the assembled journalists were given the details. Apparently, Wolf Quasner had hoped to sell the story for a six-figure sum in marks, and had apparently done business both with the *Daily Mail* and Independent Television News. At any rate, the story was swallowed hook, line and sinker.

Until, that is, initial doubts began to surface in a local newspaper on 5 August. Dr Hildebrandt admitted that he had suspicions, because the video film only showed the car actually driving about in West Berlin and not emerging from the checkpoint. In addition, an enterprising reporter had checked with the customs at the Invalidenstrasse who told him that they entered the numbers of every Soviet car that passed through in a special book. On the given date, no Lada had been registered with that particular number. It also transpired that the Allies had interrogated Braun during the course of the weekend and that the West Berlin CID wished to interview him.

The fact that the escape was a fake was revealed the following morning in one of the sensational West Berlin newspapers. They had been contacted by a self-employed car painter who felt that he could no longer remain silent in view of all the publicity. He told a reporter that some two weeks earlier he had been asked secretly to respray a Lada, and had looked for suitable premises. When he had managed to rent a garage, the car was brought to him, together with a three-litre can of synthetic paint, identical to the BMW Puzta Green. The newspaper even discovered where the paint had been purchased and the salesman readily identified Quasner who, as a regular customer, had been given a discount.

By this stage Dr Hildebrandt, who is a highly respected figure in West Berlin, had to agree that he had been fooled and that he would have to suffer the consequences. He was prepared to tender his resignation of the *Arbeitsgemeinschaft* at a special members' meeting. Hildebrandt did, however, make the point that he had worked together with Wolf for many years and had never had any reason to doubt him. All his previous escapes, of which there had been many, had always proved to be genuine.

The following day there were further revelations, when the same newspaper discovered a secondhand dealer who specialised in militaria. He admitted having provided Wolf Quasner with the necessary badges and hats, and added that the gentleman had been for years a valued customer. The dealer was told that a film was being made and was even invited to watch the crew at work. One evening, Wolf picked him up and took him to the Bernauerstrasse where he found eight people clustered around a camera, all of whom spoke only English. It was also revealed that the flats of both Quasner and Braun had been broken into by the police and searched, in the absence of the owners who had gone to ground. Thereby certain items had been confiscated pending eventual charges being preferred. The West Berlin counter-intelligence authorities admitted that during an interrogation Braun had made a complete confession, in an attempt to free himself from suspicion that he was an agent of the East German State Security Service. It was established that he had genuinely been helped to escape by Quasner on 16 June, but the rest had been a pack of lies from start to finish. Both men were to be prosecuted for such crimes as impersonating an officer and forgery, but charges of fraud were dropped when it was discovered that the various media clients had paid advance sums into an escrow account and not directly to Quasner himself. He stated publicly that he had intended to return the money after the 13 August anniversary and to confess the deception. The author's own interpretation is as follows. Wolf had a good record as an escape helper although he has his detractors, and decided to pull a stunt. When the original plan went wrong, he found himself in the position of having told everyone that he was going to produce a spectacular rabbit out of a hat, and could not deliver. In desperation, he dreamed up the trick with the shop window dolls and hoped to get away with it, at least until the anniversary was over and media interest in the Berlin Wall had subsided. He was accused in the papers of wearing a 30,000 DM diamond ring and of being always after money, yet he drives a secondhand Mercedes that has seen better days and lives in a comfortable yet not opulent flat in an unfashionable area of the city. One is inclined to give him the benefit of the doubt and credit for his certain successes.

9

Recent Years

We have seen that in the case of the major escape helpers, the ever increasing sophistication of the border defences forced them to look further afield for softer options. The same applied to many would-be escapees who planned their bids without helpers from the West. Czechoslovakia and Hungary were always favourites, followed by Romania. By the 1980s, such routes had become so popular that elements of farce could creep into events that so often ended tragically. When the author was in West Berlin in 1986, he spoke at length to a number of young people who had just arrived in the city, having been ransomed by the West German government from prison in the East. One told me that he had decided to attempt to escape and picked on the Czech border with Austria. He equipped himself as if for a hiking tour and made his way perfectly legally towards the frontier area, only entering the prohibited zone at night. Unsure of his exact whereabouts and guided only by a compass, he came to the floodlit border strip and hid in some bushes to time the patrols. Very scared, he waited, only to be startled by the sound of crunching twigs and stealthy movements. Expecting to be caught anyway, he decided to reveal himself and surrender, rather than risk being shot – only to discover that he was giving himself up to two other equally frightened youths from the same suburb of East Berlin.

In the end they tossed up for who should make the first attempt and all were caught by Czech border guards. Taken to the nearest headquarters, they expected to be beaten up, but instead were questioned by a bored captain and given food and a bed in the cells. He told them that the capture of East Germans was so commonplace in his sector that he wished they would choose somewhere else. Taken later to Prague they were placed in a train compartment for East Berlin that was reserved every Friday for returning the week's 'bag'. It was only when they were received at the East German border by the State Security officers that their troubles really began.

Even so there were still brave or foolhardy people, depending on your point of view, who were prepared to risk the defences of the Wall itself, and who in a trickle every year, made good their way to freedom. What had to be remembered is that for every successful escape, an unknown number of others were foiled, often when still in the planning stage. Escape attempts are never publicised in the East German press, and thus the casualty list can only be guessed at. A fusillade of shots in the night, heard by patrolling policeman. A limp body being carried away by *Grepos*. A snippet of information from a defector. These are the sources used by the authorities in the West in compiling their statistics. As we consider some of the happy endings in this chapter, we should remember those brave people who tried and failed.

One of the most powerful motivations for the human soul is love, which can transcend all fears of personal risk. In 1976, a Syrian businessman named Alfine Fouad was a regular visitor to East Berlin, where he met and fell in love with Elke Kohler, a divorcee with two young children. Fouad himself, as a foreigner, could legally cross to and from the West and each time he passed through Checkpoint Charlie he registered every detail of the routine followed by the duty guards. One factor that his keen eye observed was that the striped pole which lifted to admit cars coming in from the West one at a time dropped again only very slowly. One morning in April he packed Elke and her children, daughter Heike aged 12 and son Thomas aged 11, in the boot of his car, a Mercedes. Cramped in the narrow dark space, they heard Fouad shut the door and start the engine, moving out into the traffic for the short run to Checkpoint Charlie.

The Mercedes drove into the checkpoint and Fouad parked there for a quarter of an hour, going nonchalantly into the foreign exchange office to establish an air of innocence. Then he moved his car towards the head of the queue and waved his papers for attention to the guards when they were busy checking other cars. But his eyes were measuring time and distance. Having manoeuvred himself quite close to the entry point, he seized his one and only chance. As a car drove in, he gunned the engine and roared under the slowly sinking barrier. The guards were too astonished to open fire and all Fouad suffered was a badly dented roof panel as he scraped through to freedom.

Another successful escape in 1976 was also via Checkpoint Charlie and relied entirely on bluff. On 23 October at half-past two in the afternoon, an American soldier in uniform walked into the East German control point. An everyday occurrence and normally he would have been simply waved through. As he was on foot, however, the guards were suspicious – US soldiers do not usually walk – and took him into the office. There they questioned him for a quarter of an hour and he replied in fluent English, which they did not understand. Finally they let him go and quite coolly he sauntered through the barriers until he crossed into the West, and asked to be taken to the police. Asked where he came from, he replied, 'I am a refugee from DDR'. When questioned as to where he obtained the uniform, he would only state that he had got it from a friend.

A few weeks later, the youngest escapee to cross the Wall arrived in the West in a hail of bullets which luckily missed the target. Like many lads of his age, 15-year-old Frank Krause had been having difficulties in school and as a result had quarrelled with his parents. Apparently on the spur of the moment he decided to flee to the West where his aunt lived. His plan was a simple one – to use a ladder to climb over. He lived in the East Berlin borough of Prenzlauer Berg and thus made his way to the nearest stretch of Wall which ran along the Bernauerstrasse. Using his ladder, young Frank clambered over the inner wall and ran across the death strip and the anti-vehicle ditch. It was only when he reached the outer wall itself that the guards in the watchtower sited some 400 metres distant noticed the slight figure of the boy. As he propped his ladder against the Wall and started to climb, they opened fire with machine pistols and let off about thirty-five rounds, all of which missed. The exhausted Frank managed to reach the pipe on the top and tumbled into the West, much to the surprise of two passers-by.

A few days after his deadly adventure, Frank passed back to the East, apparently of his own free will. In a press statement the West Berlin youth authority made the point that children over 14 years old can decide for themselves on which side they wish to live. Frank, after lengthy discussions, had wished to return home and face the inevitable music.

One of the many anomalies of Berlin is the S-bahn railway system, mainly overground, but running partly through tunnels. Started in 1882, it was rapidly expanded throughout the greater Berlin area and was electrified in the early 1930s. After the war, the Allies left the whole system in the hands of the *Reichsbahn* whose headquarters were in the East and who continued to run it. In 1949, staff living in West Berlin went on strike for 38 days as they no longer wanted to be paid in East-Marks. There were running fights at the stations resulting in one thousand injured and two dead – but the strikers won their point. The truncated system even survived the building of the Wall in spite of a general boycott of what was known as 'Ulbricht's rattletrap' by the Berliners. Almost empty, the vintage red and cream rolling stock with the slatted wooden seats rattled through weed-infested half-ruined stations. Since early 1984, however, the S-bahn system has always had a fascination for would-be escapers, being one of the few bridges between the divided city. The S-3 line runs overground from Friedrichstrasse in the East to Charlottenburg in the West and gives a fascinating view close-up of the Wall fortifications. This trip is said to be popular with West Berlin alcoholics who can use the DDR duty-free shop in Friedrichstrasse station. The S-2 line runs from Anhalter Bahnhof in the West to Lichtenrade via a number of closed stations under the centre of East Berlin. All you can see are the dimly lit platforms patrolled usually by a *Volkspolizist* with machine pistol at the ready.

One of the lines running in the East passes extremely close

to the Wall near the Bornholmerstrasse crossing point. In broad daylight in May 1977, an 18-year-old East Berliner pulled the emergency brake. As the train juddered to a halt, he sprang out, clambered over a barbed-wire fence and a 6-foot high wall, before landing in the French Sector with only a few grazes to show for his daring. He had been a regular traveller on the line and had noted that the section between two stations could not easily be overlooked by the watchtowers.

The following story illustrates the risks involved. Rainer Pekar was 24 years old when he finally managed to escape, having already served two sentences in prison for failed attempts. After his last spell inside Rummelsberg Prison for 'attempted unlawful frontier crossing' he was placed under state observation. This meant that he could no longer work at his trade, was given a job working a sewing machine and had to live in a bed-sitter to which the local police had a key. He was subject to controls at any time of the night or day.

On the night of 23/24 May 1977, accompanied by a friend called Uwe, Rainer Pekar managed to get into a courtyard abutting on to the Wall in the Bernauerstrasse. 'Then we climbed over the first wall and scrambled over the electric fence in the death strip. Both of us had already reached the final wall when shots rang out. I felt impacts beside me and then I tumbled over into the West. Uwe had disappeared. I just heard him call out, "It's over, get going". I believe that he was hit.' We do not know what happened subsequently to Uwe, whether he lived or died.

That is one aspect of the price of freedom. Others have resorted to trickery and cunning on the Machiavellian principle that the ends justify the means. A certain East Berliner due to start a 20-month prison sentence for 'theft of state property' asked a friend in the West to pay him a visit. The friend duly came over and the would-be refugee used the occasion to steal his papers – one of the oldest tricks in the book. Rapidly changing his hair style, he crossed into West Berlin via the Friedrichstrasse S-bahn line and gave himself up to the police, leaving his friend in dire trouble. In such cases the *Vopos* are naturally suspicious of a plot and usually hold a Westerner for several weeks in prison and under interrogation, before they let him or her go.

Another cool but hardly moral trick was used by two East Berliners who had made the aquaintance of the Chancellor of the Belgian Embassy to the DDR. They visited the Belgian and slipped a powerful sleeping draught into his drink. When he duly passed out they took his diplomatic passport and changed the photograph, stole his car keys and made their way to Checkpoint Charlie. One of the refugees drove while the other hid under the rear seat. At the checkpoint, the guards take little notice of cars with diplomatic plates and so the two passed through without hindrance, leaving their unfortunate host with a bad head and a lot of explaining to do.

1978 was a vintage year for escapes over the Berlin Wall and the year got off to a good start. Late on New Year's Eve, a couple were celebrating in their flat in Buckow, when they heard the bell ring. At the door was 37-year-old Paul Konig, who said that he had just climbed over the wall and wanted to go to the Ernst Reuter Platz. It transpired that the man had been a political prisoner for four years in the DDR and had simply assumed that on New Year's Eve, the guards would be less attentive. In February, a man of the same age, Werner Arenthold, made an equally daring and successful attempt. He was working with a team of gardeners in the death strip, sowing grass seed, and seizing his opportunity when the attention of the guards was diverted, clambered onto a bulldozer and from there managed to get over the Wall. Tumbling down on the Western side, he broke his foot.

Lying injured but in freedom, Arenthold was discovered by two young boys who alerted the police and an ambulance. In an interview from his hospital bed, he emphasised that he had not left behind a wife or children. He said, 'I have been waiting since 1971 for this chance and therefore have not taken on any family ties.' He belonged to a small circle of trusted workers who were allowed into the prohibited zone, although he had never joined the Communist Party. Yet three years before he had failed to vote in an election and as a result had not been allowed to work in the vicinity of the Wall. 'I had given up all hope of escape, but then someone on high must have been asleep. At the beginning of the year I was detailed off for work again in the prohibited zone.'

If you cannot tunnel under the Wall or climb over it easily, one answer is to fly over. This occurred to two brothers in their twenties, both of whom were engineers and members of the DDR *Gesellschaft fur Sport und Technik*. This is a para-military Party-run organisation which among other activities organises flying lessons. The brothers decided to take such a course and progressed as far as solo landings and take-offs in a Czech Zllin trainer, at the Schonhagen airfield, only ten minutes flying time away from West Berlin. One Sunday in April, the younger of the two took up the machine and made two circuits so as to allay suspicion. Then just before the third take-off, his brother, who had hidden himself near the runway, scrambled in and off they went at tree-top height. In spite of orders from the control tower to land, they crossed the wall and set down on the runway of the British base at Gatow.

One might assume that those set to guard the Wall are all hand-picked 100 per cent Communists trusted by the authorities and prepared to shoot to kill. The problem is that the frontier fortifications are so extensive both around Berlin and between the DDR and West Germany, that conscripts have to be used. There are simply not enough absolute supporters of the regime to ensure that the *Grepo* troops are all reliable. There is an old joke which asks why the guards patrol in threes. The answer is that the first one can read, the second can write, and the third is there to watch two dangerous intellectuals.

Andreas Puttlich spent his period of military service guarding the Wall between November 1975 and April 1977, using the long hours of boredom to speculate on possible ways of getting over. The son of a teacher, he had grown up in Ebersbach in the DDR together with his close friend Michael Hutter, listening to Western pop music and feeling confined. After his period in the forces, Andreas went to Greifswald to study dentistry and Michael to East Berlin to study medicine, but the two kept in touch and discussed plans to escape. Starting in January 1978, Andreas travelled each weekend to Berlin to perfect their plans, but then a problem intervened, in the shape of 20-year-old Ricci Wagner, a fellow student of

Michael's. They had fallen in love and naturally she wanted to go too, which involved a lot of rethinking.

The actual plan relied on Andreas' knowledge of the guard system along the Wall and the basic fear that the lower ranks had when confronted by officers. The three youngsters were well aware that if caught they would spend ten years in prison, as well as running the risk of being shot during the actual attempt. The first problem was the necessary equipment. They managed to obtain a pair of bolt cutters and officers' uniforms were mocked-up out of ordinary clothing. The caps were stolen from the cloakroom at the University during a lecture for army doctors, and folding ladders were manufactured secretly, short enough to fit inside a Wartburg car. One Sunday they drove to the vicinity of the Wall at Babelsberg to find out the number combinations on the registration plates of *Grepo* cars, and also made up the necessary bridging cables to short-circuit the signal wires in the death strip.

Using their student grants which were paid out in June, they rented a white Wartburg with Babelsberg number plates, so that it would not be remarked on when being driven around the area. They made three attempts, but each time lost their nerve. With money dwindling the three youngsters realised they had only one more chance and rented the car for the last time. The following account of the actual attempt is taken from an interview which the trio gave to the magazine *Quick*.

Our fourth attempt started on 18 July. At six in the morning Andreas picked up the Wartburg from Babelsberg and collected the other two from the student hostel where they lived. With our last money we bought a tin of beef soup, and sat there spooning it in, feeling very wretched. Everything was checked over once again – from the bolt cutters to the sausage that Ricci had bought for the guard dogs on the border. Then we set off with all the papers and documents that could be of use to us in the West.

We parked at the place where we were going to risk our escape, until midnight, watching how the patrols entered the prohibited zone and whether they came out again. For a variety of reasons the situation seemed to us to be too uncertain and we broke off the attempt. At half past three we were back in Berlin, so depressed that our feelings were impossible to describe. But before we went to sleep, we promised each other that we would have another go.

The following afternoon we were back in position and watched the patrols, Michael and Ricci disguised as lovers. . . . It was around midnight that the coast was finally clear. We changed into our uniforms and threw our clothes into the woods. The number plates of the Wartburg were removed and we fitted a home-made one to the rear – officers' cars do not have plates at the front. Then we drove to the gate in the inner wall through which we would enter the prohibited zone. Ricci was hidden behind the seats. Giving the correct horn signal and switching off the headlights, Michael got out and cut the padlock chain of the gate. Andreas drove through and Michael fastened the gate from the inside with a new lock and chain that we had brought with us.

We drove off along the patrol road and there in front was the first watchtower, 200 metres away. We blinked the lamps twice which in the Army means 'everything OK'. Our car and the signal had the desired effect – the soldiers didn't trust themselves to open fire on this unannounced officers' visit. . . . We drove off quickly and there was the tree. We had reached the dead ground between two watchtowers. We clamped the cable to short out the signal wire and Michael cut through it. Only 2 metres to the Wall. We unfolded our ladders and propped them against it. Michael and Ricci cried out, 'There are the railway tracks'. They were the tracks leading to freedom for on the other side lay the West Berlin enclave of Steinstucken. Jumping down from the Wall, Ricci sprained her hand. Andreas got caught and ripped a few buttons off his trousers. The hats we lost anyway. When we reached the road that lay in the West, we hugged each other. Yes, we were in the West.

These three brave youngsters had managed to beat the system at its own game, and had chosen a weak spot in the Wall

135

defences. Steinstucken is a small area of West Berlin territory some 500 metres inside the DDR. It is joined to the West by a narrow finger of land walled on either side. Parallel runs a railway line from Drewitz into West Berlin, and an opening in any wall is an inherent weakness. This was used in October 1979 by two 21-year-old students from Halle. One made it, but the other fell behind and was arrested. The two managed to clamber over a wall bordering the railway track just at the moment when a slow-moving goods train blocked the view of the nearby watchtower. Sadly, however, they mistimed their attempt and one of them was too late. The other managed to grab the buffer of the rear wagon and was dragged several hundred metres until he was able to run into Steinstucken. There he made his way to the bus stop minus his shoes which had been pulled off. The bus driver said afterwards: 'I had six passengers on board. At the stop an elderly couple and another man were waiting, and then came the refugee. I said to him, "Lie down in the gangway". The rest of the passengers sat themselves around him so that he was well hidden.'

A few months earlier there had been a similar escape, in exactly the same place. Hans-Dieter Vollbracht had already made a previous attempt whereby he had been caught 3 kilometres before the Yugoslav frontier and had had to serve three years in prison. Afterwards he was placed under police supervision and was likely to be visited in his flat at any time of the day or night. It was such pressures that forced him to make another try, and one day just after midnight, he slipped out of the block and made his way on foot to Drewitz beside the railway line. As a goods train approached, he climbed over the fence and forced his way through three layers of barbed wire, only to fall foul of the fakir's mat. This consisted of 1-metre-wide boards placed on the ground with pointed nails sticking out of them, one of which went through his left foot. In spite of the injury he ran after his train, but with 100 metres still to go he heard a shout for him to stop. While he was running for his life the shots smacked into the wall beside him, but then he was into Steinstucken and safety.

Later he said: 'I am happy to be in freedom at last. I haven't got any silly ideas in my head. I know that one has to work here too. But one thing I do know. Here you get something in return and can live your life without political force and State terror.'

The possibilities seem endless. Gliders, trains, diplomatic cars and light aircraft. Yet another aspect of the geography of Berlin that we have touched on before is the fact that the city is criss-crossed by waterways, two rivers, lakes and a system of canals. All these are well patrolled, the frontiers are well marked by buoys when they run in the middle of the stream, and generally swimmers are highly visible. But imagine the surprise of the bus driver on Line 28 in West Berlin as he waited to leave on a journey into the city centre from Kreuzberg. Someone knocked on the closed bus door and the driver saw a frogman, complete with wet suit, flippers and oxygen tank, his goggles in his hand. He said, 'I've just come from the East. Can you drive me to the police, please.' The astonished driver went to a telephone and rang the police, who thought that he was having them on. Somewhat irritated the police patrol arrived to find the bus driver and a frogman.

The escape was an extremely chancy operation, as the man had to make his bid in the dark and had to rely on his sense of direction for the underwater swim in the inky blackness of the River Spree. In the late evening on a Thursday in September 1979, he managed to slip into the river at a point some 400 metres away from the entrance to the Landwehr Canal, which lies in West Berlin. Swimming some 2 metres under the water he felt his way along the metal grid which is planted in the middle of the river, until he was opposite the watchtower parallel to the canal entrance. There he sank down to the bottom at 8 metres in depth, and blind, swam for the lock gate leading into the canal. It was only after he reached the gate at the far end that he knew he was in the West and was able to surface. Once out of the water he had only to clamber over a low wall and walk dripping to the bus stop.

1980 was a fairly quiet year for escapes. In February, two youths managed to abseil down from the newspaper building right next to Checkpoint Charlie, only a few metres from the place where Peter Fechter was killed. In April, escape helpers broke open a doorway through the Wall and a young couple

137

ran across the death strip, uninjured by the hail of bullets fired after them. In September there was a further success over one of the most closely guarded sections of the Wall in the city centre, again with the aid of organisers in the West. One of the helpers climbed into the roof of St Michael's Church while the others waited with ladders beside the Wall. On the other side were two young East Berliners with a ladder which they had stolen from a building site. According to accounts at the time, the nearest watchtower was unoccupied. The man on the roof gave the signal and the two refugees climbed over the inner wall and rushed across the death strip, while at the same time, the helpers in the West pushed a ladder over the outer Wall. A few shots were fired, but a machine pistol from 400 metres is hardly accurate. The two got over safely and were rushed away in a car by their helpers. Two months later another two managed to get over the Wall at Fronau in the north, but at least one other companion was left behind, hit by several shots.

It is easy to read about these brave attempts while sitting comfortably in the freedom of a Western country, and it is safe to say that this book will never be generally available in the public libraries of the East. Only someone who has been to Berlin and has actually looked at the Wall and its defences can really imagine the difficulties and the extraordinary courage required to make a bid for freedom. In January 1981, a young couple dared and were successful. They waited and waited for a foggy day and when at last they were satisfied that the fog was thick enough, they calmly went to work as usual. Jorg Minnich was a building machinery fitter and his wife Gabriele worked in a bank. After work they took a tram to a point near the Wall at Rosenthal, north of the actual city. There they waited until the evening. Then they managed to get over the 3.5-metre-high inner wall and into the death strip, hidden by fog. Jorg cut the alarm signal wires and immediately the night was filled by the howling of the sirens. But they ran on over the anti-vehicle obstacles and got to the outer wall, which at that place was in the form of a mesh fence. At that stage the first guards appeared and Jorg almost threw his wife over, having agreed beforehand that she was not to wait for him. Jorg himself ran off through the fog along the fence as the first shots rang out, and after about 100 metres, scrambled over with bullets flying around him. By a miracle he was not hit. His wife meanwhile had run towards a bus stop and persuaded a driver to call the police, while Jorg flagged down a passing car. It was only at the police station that they were reunited. The story of a simple couple, which was worth two short columns in a Berlin newspaper.

In September of the same year, two East German border guards fled to West Berlin after they had locked one of their comrades into the watchtower where they had been on duty. They arrived in Lichtenrade in full uniform and still carrying their weapons. Just two more to join the list of DDR troops who chose to cross over and were able to make use of their privileged positions.

In 1976, Karl-Friedrich Fenk was legally allowed a move to West Germany, but as a result, his brother Hans-Jurgen was not permitted to take his final exams as an agricultural engineer. As a potentially 'unreliable' person he was subjected to repeated interrogations by the State Security police. In the meantime he married a doctor, Eveline, and both decided to escape. They made their plans during secret meetings in Czechoslovakia with their brother who, for the purpose, landed himself a job as a long-distance lorry driver with a West Berlin firm in September 1980. The escape party was to consist of Hans-Jurgen and his wife, their 3-year-old son, and a friend, Winfried Kretschmar. Karl Friedrich, as a trusted employee, started to make regular runs into the DDR with a 38-ton articulated rig and he prepared a secret entrance into the trailer which had to be reached from underneath, so as not to disturb the customs' seals at the rear.

The rendezvous was timed for 2 o'clock in the morning at kilometre 212 on the transit autobahn near Armstadt. In bitterly cold snowy weather the escapers drove in their Skoda to the agreed meeting point where they had to hang around for more than an hour. Then the lorry arrived and it took only two minutes to climb inside through the secret hatch. For another three and a half hours they huddled together inside in the bitter cold before reaching the border where they had to wait to be checked through. It was then that disaster nearly struck, as their little son suddenly began to scream. His mother tried to muzzle him as the others threw coats over them to stifle the row. But luckily, when the DDR officials arrived to check the trailer, the little boy was silent. A few minutes afterwards they rolled through the West Berlin Checkpoint and into freedom. From there, released from their prison, they did a lap of honour in the lorry down the Kurfurstendamm, equipped only with a plastic bag of documents and some baby clothes. The only problem was that the brother who had driven the truck was immediately sacked without notice, as his employers wished to distance themselves from the operation.

After each attempt, the East Berlin authorities inspected the scene of the escape and were constantly working to improve weak points but still people managed to get through. In January 1982, a 24-year-old East Berliner, who had been planning to escape for several years, made his way by tram to the Chausseestrasse, where the actual wall is fronted by the rails of the S-bahn which is still within DDR territory. He took with him an opera glass, and gaining access to a block of flats bordering the Wall, observed the patrols through the windows looking out from the staircase. Waiting until a patrol had passed, he ran out of the house just after midnight, got up on to a fence and from there on to the actual Wall. He then carefully dropped down and lay between the tracks, clutching in his hand a lucky talisman, a tiny pig on a chain. Lying there in the dark he could clearly see the guards in the watchtower, smoking and chatting, and after about fifteen minutes he began to crawl inch by inch out of their line of fire. When he felt safe he scrambled down the embankment into West Berlin territory and stopped a passing car, the driver of which refused to believe his story and drove on. Finally he came upon a Turk who called a taxi and drove him to the police station.

In September of the same year there was another escape in the same area. At around midnight a West Berlin railway worker was walking along the S-bahn track checking for damage, when suddenly he heard shots. Casting around in the dark he found a young man lying near the Wall with a hand injury, who was so tense that he could only stutter. What had happened was that two teenage lads had managed to get across the death strip to the foot of the outer wall. One cupped his hands to give the other a lift on to the top of the wall and the latter made it. As he leant down to grab his friend, guards opened fire. The lucky one tumbled down into the West having seen that the other had been badly hit. A routine protest was made by the French sector commandant to the DDR authorities about the use of firearms, which as usual remained unanswered.

The most spectacular escape in recent years took place at the beginning of April 1983 and had been planned beforehand for several months. A 23-year-old heating installer, Michael Becker, and a 24-year-old friend, decided to escape on New Year's Eve, and spent several weeks driving as near to the Wall as possible in a rented Wartburg, looking for a suitable spot. The method they planned was the old high wire trick which had been used before. They also made contact with a helper in the West, without whom that particular method cannot work.

Finally they narrowed their choice down to a five-storey apartment block in the Schmollerstrasse, occupied mainly by frontier troops as it lay right against the Wall. Thirty metres away was the Bouchestrasse in the West, also with tall blocks of flats, one of those Berlin streets where inhabitants on both sides of the Wall can see into each others' living rooms. Between them, however, lie the death strip, bunkers, watchtowers and vehicle obstacles as well as the ever present Wall itself. In fact the pavement of the Bouchestrasse, which is all that is left as the Wall runs along the gutter, is still Eastern territory although one can walk along it.

As all those in the Schmollerstrasse house were in employment, the building was empty at midday. Michael Becker and his friend drew up outside the house one Thursday, wearing blue workmens' overalls, and quite coolly carried a number of oddly shaped items inside, transporting them up to the spacious loft. The equipment consisted of a fibre-glass bow and two arrows, a 100-metre length of nylon fishing line, a 90-metre long, 34-kilo steel cable, 6 millimetres thick, a mountaineer's carabina hook and two rollers fitted with hand grips. For more than fifteen hours the men waited hidden in the loft. Then at 5 o'clock the following morning they fastened one end of the cable around a massive chimney stack and the other end to the fishing line. Michael Becker then took the bow and at a signal from their helper on the other side, fired an arrow right over the roof of the house opposite. There it was caught and the steel cable was pulled over the death strip and down into a courtyard where the end was tied to a car which was then driven forward to provide the necessary tension. It is probable that the guards in the nearby watchtower had nodded off, as otherwise they could hardly have failed to see that stage of the operation. Once the cable was tight, each trip on the roller took only a matter of seconds. Michael and his friend were deposited sprawling on the opposite roof after their 30-metre crossing and managed to climb into the loft through a hatch. Both said afterwards that they had not dared to look down.

At the end of 1983, the West Berlin rugby club gained a useful new member who had played for the DDR in international matches, the 23-year-old Burt Weiss. Regarded as 'politically unreliable', he had not been selected recently, which was hardly surprising as he had already made several unsuccessful applications for an exit visa, and exactly a year before had failed in an escape bid. A superbly fit young man, Burt Weiss had chosen to swim to freedom but had to do so in the freezing cold of winter as he needed the protection of fog. In the 1982 attempt he had touched an alarm wire and had been shot at by police patrol boats but had luckily been able to get back on land unobserved.

He chose virtually the same spot as the frogman mentioned earlier, but Burt's equipment was not so sophisticated – he had only a wet suit and a home-made snorkel with which to make a 2.5-kilometre swim and without the ability to dive deep. He slipped into the River Spree one evening at half-past eight and covered the first 300 metres just underwater, swimming slowly so to create as little disturbance as possible. Then came the really dangerous part. There was a metal fence right across the river, anchored into the bed and sticking out above the water some 2.5 metres high, and a watchtower at either end. Burt slid gently into the shore and crawled on land, where he had to get through a narrow gap between the fence and the Wall, right at the base of the tower. Managing this, he slipped back into the icy water and passed another tower whose searchlight was playing over the surface of the water. At this stage he had been already three hours immersed and was thoroughly frozen. Burt remembered thinking that he would not hear any warning shout, and if seen would be shot. During the fourth hour of the trip there was a final obstacle. He had to swim directly under a landing stage that was patrolled by guards and was covered by a further series of watchtowers. But then, after a short pause, he knew that there was only another 200 metres between himself and freedom, where the Wall bent away from the river bank at the entry to the Landwehr Canal. The ordeal ended when he scrambled ashore in the Schlesischestrasse and saw cars with West Berlin plates and an Aral filling station. He waved down a car driven by a Turk, who before driving him to the police, took him to his local pub for a drink.

A few weeks later another very lucky swimmer made it, a 17-year-old who picked a spot at the south-west corner of Berlin where the River Havel, some 200 metres wide, forms the frontier. One lunchtime on a cold January day, two anglers were sitting on the West Berlin shore waiting for a bite, and as they looked across the river, they saw a refugee come shinning over the Wall on the opposite bank, carrying a suitcase. The actual water temperature was only five degrees, yet the refugee slipped into the river and started swimming with only one arm – the other one he used to clutch his case. About half way across he started to get into difficulties and cried out for help, but luckily the nearest watchtower was unoccupied because of building work. The anglers yelled at him to keep going and finally managed to reach him with a life ring which they used to pull him to the shore. On land and in safety, the youngster could not walk. The anglers carried him to a nearby restaurant, where one of the waiters stripped him naked and dumped him under a warm shower. The lad was wearing only an overall, pullover and cord trousers although he had wrapped bandages for warmth around his stomach and wrists. He was suffering from exposure but the fire brigade drove him to hospital where he quickly recovered.

Many of the escapes which have been described were the result of accurate planning using outside help and involving

143

quite complicated equipment. Others seem to have been solo efforts dreamed up on the spur of the moment. In October 1984, another 17-year-old lad was feeling fed up with life, lack of opportunities and the ever prevalent black market and petty corruption in the DDR. One day after finishing work, he wandered around for a while and then took the train into the centre of East Berlin. Standing on the Alexanderplatz he found himself dreaming of the Kurfurstendamm in the West and made up his mind to escape. Still without any real idea of what was involved he made his way to the vicinity of the crossing point at the Sonnenalle. As he said afterwards, 'there were three possibilities. Either I would get away with it, or they catch me, or they gun me down.' At that point on the East German side there is an area of allotments and garden houses, popular with Berliners at the weekends. The impromptu refugee hid himself in the undergrowth for six hours before discovering a ladder. Laying his leather jacket over the barbed wire on top of the inner wall, he climbed over, pulled the ladder after him and crouched inside the death strip. Getting across nearly cost him his life, as he must have touched the alarm signal wires. Just as he was going up the ladder to get over the outer wall, a salvo of shots was fired from the nearby watchtower. The youngster, thoroughly frightened, then fell from the top of the Wall into the West, breaking his ankle in the process. While all this was going on, a postman who lived on the Western side in a house close to the Wall was jerked out of his sleep by the noise of firing. Hearing the sound of broken glass, his first thought was burglary but then he realised that the shots came from the Wall. Looking out he saw the refugee at the bottom of the Wall and shouted to him 'You are in the West. Quick. Come over to the house.' While they were sitting in the kitchen over a glass of beer, it was at first thought that the injury was a simple sprain, but X-rays at the hospital revealed broken bones.

That young man was one of the lucky ones. Six weeks after his escape, a further fusillade was heard during the night. After about an hour, West Berlin police and a French gendarmerie patrol observed a lifeless body being taken away in a DDR military vehicle.

One thing is certain, however, that as long as the Wall exists, there will be courageous people prepared to risk their lives to cross it. The last escape from Berlin at the time the necessary research was completed, took place at the beginning of 1986. At that time, the East German side of Checkpoint Charlie was being modernised and a whole gang of workmen had been busy for several weeks, carefully guarded by armed frontier police. As a result of the building work, the telephone cables had to be relaid, which was the responsibility of 23-year-old Andreas Bratke who had been working there for three weeks. Each day he watched out for a chance but had more or less given up hope even though he could see the Western control point only 100 metres away. The guard attached to him would not take his eyes off him for a minute. But when it came to the last afternoon on the last day of the job, Andreas realised that it was then or never. Using a temporary distraction as his opportunity, he dropped his tools and ran, partly covered by a car that was just leaving the checkpoint. But then he was in the open and expecting every second to be shot. The guard ran after him, shouting 'I'll get the pig', but did not open fire, and stopped when he got to the actual frontier. Totally exhausted, Andreas collapsed and was dragged into the Customs post on the Western side, from where he was rushed off to hospital and put under sedation. Later he said that during the brief run he had felt the impact of a bullet between the shoulder blades. The reason that no shots were fired may have been because there were a large number of witnesses on the Western side. It was certainly not because of a change of heart by the East Berlin regime.

This chapter ends on a note of mystery. In July 1986, reports started to surface in West German newspapers of a shoot-out in the underground system below the Eastern part of the city. What is certain is that the Alexanderplatz station and nearby shops were closed on 7 May and evacuated for several hours. The reason given was a subway fire. Persistent rumours, however, pointed to a dramatic but tragic escape bid that went seriously wrong. Apparently, twelve would-be escapers, most of whom were army reservists from a crack unit, commandeered an empty underground train from a siding. From there they drove it to a place in the system under the city where, by operating a set of points, the track can be diverted into the West. The problem was that beyond the points was a set of heavy steel doors, which the escapers seemingly tried to ram or blow up. It was at this stage that frontier guards, who had been warned of the plot, opened fire. A regular battle took place in the tunnel which led to the death of six of the refugees and some of the guards. The remaining six were supposedly taken to a military garrison, court-martialled and shot by a firing squad. What really happened will probably never be established, as the reports were condemned as a 'foul lie' by the East German foreign ministry.

34. *Peter safe in Berlin.*

35. *Bernauerstrasse today.*

36. *Memorials to just some of those who failed to escape.*

10

The Price of Failure

The successful escapes are the ones which have tended to hit the headlines over the years – the more spectacular the method, the more column inches have been devoted to it. In addition, publicity has tended to be determined by the political climate as the press generally reflects the views of its readers or watchers. For a couple of years after the building of the Wall, escapes were big news and the escape helpers were heroes. During the period of the Social-Liberal coalition in Germany and the policy of détente, such activities tended to be played down although the ransoming of political prisoners was instituted, much to the profit of the foreign exchange account of the DDR. In more recent times, with a conservative government in Bonn and Reaganite attitudes in the USA, a more realistic view of the Communist regime in the East has been taken. The 25th anniversary commemoration revived interest in the subject for a few months.

The term 'political prisoner' is a tricky one to define. The IRA murderer and the Palestinian terrorist would both stoutly maintain that when caught, they are political prisoners. One man's freedom fighter is another's assassin. Certainly nobody would deny the right of an individual state to make laws for its own protection and to defend those laws if necessary, but there are basic human rights that have been internationally accepted. One of these rights is the freedom to travel and another is freedom of speech. If a nation which claims legitimacy denies such basic rights, then outsiders equally have the right to protest. International disfavour is rightly heaped upon South Africa, yet the world community treats Russia and its satellites with kid gloves. Russian tanks have been used to keep Hungary, the DDR, Czechoslovakia and Poland in check but protests from the West have been short-lived. Budapest in 1956, Berlin in 1961, Prague in 1968 and Warsaw in 1981 have been rapidly banished from our consciousness as we pour out our sympathy for the unfortunate black South Africans. That is small consolation for those who linger in the Gulag or serve their time in the prisons and labour camps of Russia's satellites. At the time the Berlin Wall was built, the DDR loudly accused West Germany of *menschenhandel* which literally means trading in human beings, in that industrialists were trying to recruit skilled workers from among the refugees. Yet for years now, the DDR has been quite cynically imprisoning its citizens on trumped-up charges which have no basis in terms of generally accepted human law, and when they have served part of their sentences, selling them to West Germany at 40,000 DM per head. This leads inevitably to the difficult question. Should the Bonn government encourage the DDR to swell its prison population in the sure knowledge that they will be handsomely rewarded? Cynics always say that when East Germany is short of foreign exchange, there is likely to be a wave of arrests.

In the previous chapters we have examined many of the successful escapes as well as indicating the price of failure, in terms of death, injury and imprisonment. The list of crimes that can be committed is a long one. Top of the list is naturally *Republikflucht* (fleeing the republic) or attempting to do so, for which you can get up to six years. Even thinking about it or making plans to flee is also punishable, as is the acquisition of equipment to be used in an attempt. Helping others to escape is a serious crime, whether or not money is involved, and even to demonstrate with a placard is classed as sedition against the state. A paradox is that 'fleeing' or 'flight' does not exist in the DDR official vocabulary. You can flee only if you are persecuted, and as nobody is persecuted in such an ideal state, you are a criminal if you attempt to leave. You have been deluded by the Western media or led astray by imperialist secret agents and so on. Orwellian 'New Speak' is used to justify the whole edifice of repression and the criminalisation of the natural desire for freedom.

The story of Matthias Bath is a demonstration of what can happen to those who fall foul of the DDR security apparatus. He spent 1197 days in prison as an escape helper before being exchanged for a spy who had been sentenced in West Germany, and after being released he set out his experiences in a book. In November 1975 he was in his last year at high school and preparing for his final examinations. He lived with his parents in West Berlin, had a solid middle-class background and was active in conservative politics via the Jungen Union, the youth wing of the Christian Democrats. Because of this he was sentimentally attached to the idea of German reunification and did not recognise the DDR as a separate state. He was approached by a certain man whom he knew as a functionary in the Jungen Union who asked him if he would be prepared to assist in an escape operation. Matthias knew that this person had himself fled from the DDR and was active in political opposition to the regime there, so the offer seemed plausible. He turned down the idea, however, as he was soon to take his exams, but agreed that at a later date he would be prepared. He well understood the risks but felt that he had to stand up and be counted. Helping someone to escape was an honourable deed and Matthias remembered a saying of Kurt Schumacher's: 'He who stays silent in the face of injustice makes himself equally guilty.' In January the following year, Matthias was again approached and after some hesitation agreed to take part. As the man who had contacted him was unable to travel in the DDR, he said that he needed politically reliable friends to assist and at no stage was any mention made of money. Matthias assumed that the escape operations being undertaken were to help those in need and who were suffering political persecution. He was told that all he had to do was to collect the refugees from where they lived, and take them to the autobahn where they would transfer to another car.

At a further meeting in March, Matthias was given the exact details of the plan, which had altered somewhat. Instead of just delivering the refugees, he was to drive the get-away car which would bring them through into the West at Helmstedt. For this purpose he would be provided with a car, an Opel, the boot of which was large enough to hold three people. One evening early in April he left home, leaving a note for his parents to be opened in case he failed to return, and drove out of Berlin and on to the transit autobahn. As per his instructions he headed for a parking place shortly after the Leipzig turnoff where he saw a red Skoda with some young people and a child standing by it. The registration number was the correct one, but to have an excuse for stopping, Matthias got out and made a short trip into the bushes. The Skoda started up and drove off, and after waiting for a while he followed it at a discreet distance before speeding up and overtaking. It was his responsibility to find a suitably deserted spot to effect the transfer and when he had done so to signal the Skoda that he was ready. This was the dangerous part of the operation but it was dark and there was little traffic about. He pulled quickly into a parking place that seemed deserted; while the car was still rolling he opened the door and the refugees, a couple and a child, scrambled into the back. It had not taken more than twenty seconds and he was sure that he had been unobserved as he pulled back out on to the autobahn. The car had been modified so that the rear seatback tipped forward and the refugees could climb into the boot. When they had crawled through and the back seat was repositioned, Matthias felt satisfaction at a useful job well done. He had been given some valium tablets for the adult passengers if they seemed nervous but they declined for themselves although the child was given a half. The rest of the trip seemed to be plain sailing and he felt quite confident as he drove into the checkpoint at Marienborn.

I passed through the first control without problem. But as I approached the second control under the roofed-in bay I saw a VW bus in front of me being examined. The driver had to open the flap at the back but was then allowed to drive off. This unexpected check made me very uneasy. I handed over my papers and then another guard appeared and told me to drive off and park on the left. Hardly had I done so when the vehicle was surrounded by frontier guards and customs men. After a few minutes I was told to switch off the engine, which I had left running to hide any unusual noises. I was asked a few questions about my journey which I answered as if it had been a normal transit trip. Then suddenly one of the guards said that I was under suspicion of having misused the transit agreement, and that I should open the boot. I did so and we saw the refugees lying there. Then I was told to shut it again and was informed that I was provisionally under arrest.

The rest of his book describes the period of remand, his farcical trial and his imprisonment in Rummelsburg. During interrogation, which lasted for several weeks, physical violence was not used, but he was cut off from the outside world. It was weeks before he was allowed to write his first letter and even longer before his parents were permitted to visit him. At the beginning there was solitary confinement and deprivation of sleep, degrading conditions and poor food. Exercise was permitted also in solitary confinement, in a walled-in compartment only the top of which was open to the sky. He was permitted to choose a lawyer from a list submitted by the interrogator, but was not permitted to discuss his case with him until the charges had been framed.

During the period of interrogation, it appeared that they knew who his contact man was and that he had probably been betrayed by the driver of the red Skoda. The worst aspect for Matthias was the fact that his captors proved to him that his political friend had accepted money from the refugees and was in the escape-helping business for commercial gain. Thus the idealistic basis for the risk he had taken was cut away from underneath him. It was quite clear that he was guilty, and a strong case was built up by the interrogators, based on his previous political activities and his known opposition to the DDR brand of socialism. The prosecution at his eventual trial demanded five years and that is what he got. His lawyer restricted himself to a thin plea for a milder sentence because of Matthias' youth and inexperience.

His period in Rummelsburg prison was not a happy one, although as a West Berliner he was in the 'foreigners' section.

This consisted of an average of three hundred men, 80 per cent of whom had been sentenced for escape helping in some form or other – the rest were there because of customs offences, traffic violations or violations of the frontier laws. They were all required to work in industrial plants within the prison and at first the scale of food depended on norm fulfilment. The conditions were, generally speaking, appalling: six men crowded into a cell, showers once a week, uneatable food and regular chicanery by the warders. Matthias spent considerable periods in solitary confinement for refusing to work, and suffered constant ill-health. He was finally exchanged in July 1979, and was driven over to West Berlin by the wife of Dr Vogel, the East Berlin lawyer who is mainly concerned with such matters.

Five years for such a crime would seem to be excessive, especially as Matthias had not become involved for monetary reward and was little more than a schoolboy. Men he met in prison who had made such runs for a fee often got off with less, but they could plead social deprivation. They were those who were hard up and answered advertisements in the newspapers for 'driver with own car required'. He spent his time only with Westerners so had no idea of the numbers of East Germans in the same prison and the percentage of them who were there for political offences. As such trials are always held in camera and are never reported in the newspapers, it is difficult to get hold of reliable facts and figures. The German branch of the International Commission for Human Rights has, however, published a booklet about penal conditions in the DDR based on a questionnaire answered in 1984 and 1985 by ransomed and recently released political prisoners. The following paragraphs are based on this reliable source.

If you are arrested in the DDR, no reason is given. Whether this happens at work or at home, officers of the Ministry for State Security, who are in civilian clothes, are extremely careful to avoid any sort of scene or chance for public protest. You are simply taken away in a plain car, to 'clear up some factual matters'. Once in a remand prison the first interrogation can last for up to twelve hours, whereby the trained questioners use the shock and disorientation of arrest. Promises and threats alternate and any statement made at that time is later used to trap the accused into contradictions. Presentation in front of a judge to legalise the remand is only after three or four days, and is a foregone conclusion anyway. The accused may select a lawyer from a list and about a month later can see him, but only to talk about any personal problems – not about the actual case. Remand prisoners must wear prison clothing and may use their own money to purchase toilet articles, cigarettes and extra food. On average the remand prisoner spends the first two months in solitary confinement, and when he is then put together with another prisoner, this may well be a stool pigeon who will report any conversations to the interrogators. The first visitor is allowed after about three months when the case has been completed, and again there is no possibility to discuss anything to do with the matter in hand. All prisoners are referred to only by a number and never see any other prisoners at all. Books are provided but bibles and prayer books are not.

About two weeks before the trial, the accused is shown a summary of the case against him, which is taken away again after he has read it. At that stage he may see his lawyer, but a defence as such is impossible. The lawyers are all Communist Party members and staunch pillars of the system – there is no cross-examining of witnesses or any attempt to disprove the prosecution's case. The defence is there only to make a plea in mitigation, and the prisoner is not given a copy of the court's decision and sentence. Shortly afterwards, he or she is transported to the prison where the sentence is to be served.

There are a considerable number of such prisons and work camps where political prisoners may be sent and, unlike the 'foreigners', those from the DDR are mixed together with criminals who are favoured by the warders. The women are sent to Hoheneck, an old castle near Stollberg, which holds about 750 prisoners, 250 of whom on average are there for political offences. The cells hold between 10 and 30 women in each with three-tier beds and primitive unscreened toilet arrangements. Showers are possible only once a week and the quality of the clothing is poor. According to the report, there is a wait of several days before the doctor can be seen and the women fear a stay in the prison hospital. Work is organised in

153

three shifts around the clock; making tights, sewing bedding and making prison clothes out of old army uniforms. Many of the products are exported to West Germany and other countries to earn foreign currency.

One of the largest prisons for men is Brandenburg, which can hold up to 500 political detainees at any one time, and in the East of the DDR is Cottbus. The following is a direct quote from the report, about the latter institution.

The complex consists essentially of two large cell blocks, two production halls, the reception block, a dining barrack, a small hospital and a separate remand prison. To hinder escapes there are barbed wire fences, alarm signal wires, dog runs, watchtowers and a 5-metre high wall. The buildings are in an extremely bad state although inhabited by 500 persons at any one time. Circa 350 of them have never committed a crime and are political prisoners. According to their sentence they will spend between one and five years there, and their average age is 29. All sections of the population are to be found in Cottbus prison, but in contrast to the world outside, there is a higher ratio of qualified skilled workers and those with university degrees.

New arrivals are first sent to the 'catacombs' which are the cellars underneath one of the blocks, where they spend the first twenty-four hours. . . . The next day the prisoner is kitted out and brought to the reception block. A senior warder whose nickname is 'red terror' prepares them for their stay in the prison in that he attempts to intimidate them and to make them unsure of themselves. At least one from each new entry group is beaten up by 'red terror'.

Prison clothing consists of worn out army uniforms. . . . After the entry procedure the prisoners are divided into work groups after about fourteen days and are sent to a 're-education area'. This is a closed-off corridor with six to eight cells. For each area an officer known as a 'Re-educator' is responsible. The cells hold nine prisoners in each, but can have up to twelve crammed in, in three-tier bunks.

The warders are equipped with dogs, rubber truncheons and handcuffs. Their behaviour is very different and usually incalculable – some carry out their duty when drunk. When searching cells they take no consideration for the prisoners' personal effects.... Work is organised in three shifts in the workshops of V.E.B. Sprela and V.E.B. Pentacon. In the latter, parts for 'Praktika' cameras are manufactured.... On average eleven prisoners share one wash basin and fourteen one toilet. The basins have only a cold water tap and shaving is mandatory. Showers are permitted once a week, and in spite of numbering, underwear gets mixed up in the laundry and is often reissued dirty.

Nobody goes hungry but the food is of low quality and often revolting. The lack of vitamins means that most prisoners can reckon with the loss of teeth.... After reporting sick, weeks can go by before the prisoner is brought before the doctor. Treatment is often wrong or not carried out at all. In emergencies that can happen in the cell, the prisoners can only hope to make themselves heard by shouting or banging. At night these efforts are usually unsuccessful....

Those serving more than two years can write three letters per month to permitted addresses, at the most two.... Visits from family members are possible every two months. The conversations are overheard and it is forbidden to speak about the crime, the lawyer or prison conditions.

And so it goes on. Prison in most countries is not designed to be pleasant. The one hope for those held in the almost medieval conditions in the DDR is when there is an 'action' and whether or not they will be included. These take place at irregular intervals when the government of East Germany has managed to make arrangements to ransom a group of prisoners. Negotiations are carried out via two lawyers in Berlin and a deal is struck. The money is handed over and a group of prisoners is transferred to Karl Marx Stadt prison, where on the day they are given their civilian clothes, personal possessions and a piece of paper informing them that they have been officially deprived of their DDR citizenship. The lucky group is then placed in an unmarked West German bus and, still accompanied by State Security officers, is driven to the frontier. The numbers of those ransomed in this way in recent years are given below.

1980	1012
1981	1440
1982	1530
1983	1127
1984	2341
1985 to July	1282

While researching in Berlin, the author was able to talk to a group of recently ransomed prisoners and others who had been permitted to leave to rejoin their families. Their personal stories are very tragic and often moving. They meet regularly at the Berlin office of the International Commission for Human Rights which is run by Frau Petra Dombrowski, wife of a young Berlin CDU politician. She herself was able to leave with her family, after her father demonstrated with a placard in sight of the Wall where he was photographed by Western journalists. One of her young protégés has a French father living in Paris, and was active in church affairs in Erfurt. Having been arrested and interrogated three times he decided to try to escape and was caught in the boot of a car at the Herleshausen Checkpoint. For this he was sentenced to three years in Cottbus, but after his father had applied pressure on the DDR through the good offices of the French Communist trade union (CGT), he was ransomed.

Another of the youngsters was also caught in a car boot attempt as he wanted to join his mother who was in the West. A girl who helps Petra in the office was smuggled out in the boot of a diplomatic car which was stopped at the border. When she was discovered inside, the guards simply reshut the lid and left her locked inside for nineteen hours. Only then was she dragged out, almost suffocated and in agony from cramped limbs and thirst. One young man got so fed up that he packed a bag one day, hitch-hiked to the border and simply asked to leave. He was promptly arrested but was awarded a very mild four months before being bought out. Then there is the story of the 16-year-old girl, whose parents decided to try to escape over the Hungarian border. All three were caught and sentenced. The father went to men's prison, and in spite of her age, the daughter was imprisoned with her mother for part of the time.

One girl the author met there was only 18 when she told him her story. Her parents wished to leave the DDR and settle in West Berlin. Her mother wrote a letter to the International Commission for Human Rights to ask them for advice about applying for an exit visa. This letter was naturally enough intercepted by the State Security Service and, as far as the DDR is concerned, it is a crime to contact such groups as the International Commission or Amnesty International. The mother was arrested and sentenced to two years for anti-state sedition, while father and daughter were placed under police supervision in their flat in East Berlin. Then, in due course, the mother was ransomed and deported to the West. Father and daughter applied to leave under the reunification of families agreement and this was granted fairly promptly, although they were only told literally at the last minute. They were given 24 hours to pack, could only take what they could carry and, as a final humiliation, were forbidden to hold a farewell party for their friends in the apartment block. So like thieves they had to steal away, as the authorities feared that a party might be used as an excuse for anti-state utterances and, anyway, might give others the same idea.

Father and daughter arrived on the S-bahn from Friedrichstrasse station, clutching their possessions in suitcases and a rucksack, but accompanied by the family dachshund who also had permission to leave. One person who did not have such permission was the girl's fiancé, a trained cook who worked in one of the better hotels in East Berlin. He put in an application to get married and to change his residence to the western half of the city. This was promptly turned down and he was sacked as being potentially unreliable. The girl told me with great sadness that he was selling sausages from a stand on the Alexanderplatz, but that she had been able to have a stolen meeting with him in Karlsbad, in Czechoslovakia, for a weekend. When I asked her what the solution was, she shrugged and then said: 'Well, he will have to commit some sort of minor political offence and be put in prison. Then we can both hope that he will be ransomed fairly soon and deported, so that we can get married here in freedom.'

11

In Conclusion

The Berlin Wall is now 25 years old. The probability is that it will still be there for the 50th anniversary, unless there is some way in which the DDR can fulfil the expectations of its citizens and earn their support. Much is made in the press these days about the wind of change blowing around Moscow, and one naturally wonders what will happen when the old guard finally dies out. Erich Honecker, the architect of the Wall, is still firmly in the saddle in East Berlin, and the clique which surround him are all products of the Stalinist era in ideological terms. They have to keep the 'workers' paradise' well fenced in, as even today there would be a mass exodus if the restrictions on travel were relaxed. The same would also apply to the other Eastern bloc states.

The West Berlin authorities today are in a strange position. The Christian Democrats are in power and many of those who hold senior positions in the party were active as escape helpers in the 1960s. Yet their attitude is now quite definitely against anyone who tries to rock the boat. The two parts of the city are coupled together by a whole complex of mutual agreements which include maintenance of the status quo. East Germany, for a handsome fee of course, disposes of West Berlin's rubbish, and a whole system of cultural contacts flourishes. As one official said, 'Berliners are Berliners'. The five offices where West Berliners can apply for day permits to cross into the East do a roaring trade and it is reckoned that 90 per cent have contacts on the other side of the Wall. They are prepared to buy an entry ticket to be able to keep in touch.

It is quite clear that the East Germans, given the circumstances of 1961, had to build the Wall. The alternative was surrender to the West which would have entailed Russian intervention, or slow economic collapse. Yet Eastern moves against West Berlin have been largely counter-productive. The blockade, for example, made the idea of a rearmed Federal Republic as a bulwark against Communist expansion a respectable one. That period also created the legend of the toughness and bravery of the Berliners themselves. Once founded, the Federal Republic profited from massive American aid – the chillier the termperature of the Cold War, the more support that was given. In order to continue to expand economically, West Germany needs détente, and it can be argued that the building of the Wall made this all possible. Previously the open border and the drain of refugees made the frontier in Berlin a running sore and constant flashpoint for international tension. The walling-in process which began in 1961 has resulted in a stabilisation of central Europe which has benefited all of us in the West – which is small consolation to those East Germans who would like to live in a free society.

One can say that the West Berliners have learned to live with the Wall and, as has been said earlier, many of them either never see it or if they do, ignore it. It is a massive tourist attraction and at intervals the authorities have built viewing platforms. All state visitors to Bonn make an obligatory visit to Berlin to have the reality of communism brought home to them. Much to the annoyance of Berlin politicians, such visits are usually scheduled for the weekend so that Bonn officials can have their free time. Small shops at the Potzdamerplatz do a roaring trade in Wall souvenirs and the tourists flock into the museum at Checkpoint Charlie. The well-meaning Dr Hildebrandt, who runs this useful information centre, is branded by many people in official positions in West Berlin as a cold-warmonger. Yet the whole message of his museum is concerned with human rights, which many politicians would prefer to ignore as they pursue their contacts on the other side of the border. They point out that through their efforts, West Berliners have profited in many ways and that today the DDR is far more amenable in such matters as family reunification and exit visas to attend family functions.

The present Wall is the so-called fourth-generation one, constructed of smooth concrete panels and with a concrete pipe on top. Work started on this replacement for the previous rough-cast concrete version in 1976 and is now more or less complete. What its creators did not envisage, however, is that it has proved to be an ideal painting surface. In some parts of the city, competent artists have been at work to create a colourful panorama of surrealistic fantasies. Sadly though, most of the rest of the Wall has been defaced with senseless graffiti, often of an obscene nature – enlivened only occasionally by a poignant comment. One reads, 'Whoever comes through here will get one mark from me' and in another place, there is a picture of a birthday cake with the inscription (in English), 'Happy 25th Birthday'.

The fact that the Wall can be ignored is largely a result of the developing traffic pattern. Once it was built, many traditional routes were simply cut off and no longer led anywhere. Drivers soon found other ways and the planners have tended to follow suit. As the city centre of West Berlin is some 2 kilometres away from the Wall, beyond the Tiergarten park an area of waste land has formed. It is only now that the city fathers are grappling with the problem of redeveloping the Potzdamerplatz area. Other areas along the Wall have tended to decay as residents who did not wish to have it in front of their noses moved out. In many cases they have been replaced by Turkish families attracted by the lower rents and the radical young who set up as squatters. A cynic could maintain that the Berlin Wall is the longest eyesore in the world, yet there are idyllic spots in the more rural parts where wildlife flourishes and where people have gardens running right up to it.

The everyday nature of the Wall can be illustrated by the story of the 17-year-old girl who sat on top of it with her boyfriend and smoked a cigarette. Manuela and Claudio went for a walk one hot August afternoon in 1984 and were looking for a quiet place to have a gossip and a smoke. They clambered up on to the top of the Wall and lit up quite happily, but their peace was suddenly disturbed by shouts of 'Hey, what are you doing up there?' Two armed frontier guards came running up and the youngsters panicked. Claudio fell into the West and Manuela tumbled down into the death strip at the feet of the *Grepos*. The girl was marched off to a jeep and driven to hospital where she was examined for injuries. Then, with not even a bruise to complain of, she was taken to a remand hostel and was interrogated for several hours by the police. It was not until the following afternoon that she was released and taken to the Oberbaumbrücke crossing point, from where she was able to telephone her parents.

The Wall has seen its share of protests, especially during the summer of 1986 when the 25th anniversary was commemorated – or celebrated – according to one's point of view. In July, another hole was blasted near Checkpoint Charlie, with a bomb made of four pounds of commercial explosive. Nobody was injured but several parked cars were damaged. On 7 August, the newspapers were full of pictures of an elderly man sitting astride the top of the Wall at the Potzdamerplatz, and attacking it with a hammer. The man in question was a 68-year-old American, John Runnings, who had fought in the Second World War. Apparently he had already been arrested by the East Germans three months earlier for urinating against the Wall. He justified his action in trying to knock it down by giving his motive as: 'non-recognition of the division of the city which had been achieved by force of arms, and non-recognition of the worldwide system of solving conflicts by military power.' Having made his protest for the cameras, he clambered down into the East sector and gave himself up to the waiting *Grepos*. After the usual questioning he was then shoved back to the West.

East Berlin celebrated the anniversary by a parade of para-military units, while in the West speeches were made condemning the futility of the Wall. There were a few minor demonstrations including an attempt to form a human chain right along the frontier. Television programmes and magazine articles repeated the history for a generation that has been born since 13 August 1961 and has grown into adulthood with no memory of the refugee streams. For a few short days the attention of the free world was focused on the Berlin Wall, and retired escape organisers and refugees were brought out to be interviewed. Everyone was naturally in agreement that it was a terrible disgrace and a declaration of moral bankruptcy on the part of the DDR rulers. But even so, it is there and likely to remain, as solid as the Great Wall of China, for as long as Western and Eastern Europe are divided into two mutually opposing ideologies. However solid it may seem, though, as long as it exists it will provide a challenge to the brave who will not accept being penned in by barbed wire and concrete. In a few years time this book will have to be revised with new chapters, because if one thing is certain, that is that people will still try to escape. As was stated by the DDR at the time the Wall was erected: 'The new protective measures will inevitably cause some inconveniences.'

But to end this book, there is a story of one man for whom the Wall has not proved to be a barrier, the so-called 'wall springer', Rainer Sturmo Wulf. He is now 33 years-old, works as a librarian and writes poetry. He has spent a fair amount of time in psychiatric care in West Berlin, where he is regarded as a 'character' and has even had a book written about his exploits, in the form of a novel. He was brought up in Babelsberg which lies in the East sector, to the south of West Berlin. This suburb is popular with true supporters of the regime who live there in neat villas with well-tended gardens. Naturally they have to have permits to reside within the prohibited zone, but the authorities were quite content with a somewhat primitive defensive line, consisting solely of a wall and without the usual trappings of death strip and alarm signal wires. As a child Wulf grew up with the presence of the Wall at the end of his parents' garden and an awareness that on the other side, in the Western suburb of Kohlhasenbruck, was an observation platform. His first contact with the other side was at the age of 13 when he made the acquaintance of the class enemy, in the shape of a girl of similar age. She would climb up on to the platform and they would converse about fashion and pop music plus a certain amount of verbal sex. By using a length of plastic drainpipe, she would supply him with cigarettes and Western magazines.

Wulf's first crossing of the Wall was made when he was 18.

He and a friend, mildly intoxicated, managed to cross the best-defended frontier in the world by means of a pole which they propped up against the 3.80-metre-high Wall in an area which was out of sight of the nearest watchtower. After a weekend spent wandering around in the West, they returned by the same route. This might well never have been discovered had the friend not been extremely fond of drink and equally fond of the daughter of the chief of police in Potsdam. She told her father, who saw it that the friend was called up into the army while Wulf had to spend six months in a labour camp. They had insulted the dignity of the socialist fatherland, and what was worse was that the friend was the nephew of a member of the politburo.

Wulf then drifted into the alternative culture of East Berlin for two years, before returning to the scene of the crime in 1974. Although his parents had been forced to move out of the Babelsberg enclave as a result of their son's activities, he found the same pole in the same place. In nineteen seconds he was over and settled down to a vague life-style in West Berlin, unable to remain at anything for very long. In 1979 he sprang out of a moving Underground train as it passed through the closed-off station under East Berlin's Rosenthaler Platz. The problem was that nobody took him seriously. While he craved attention, the DDR authorities saw him as a madman and promptly deported him back to the West in a Red Cross ambulance – which delivered him to a mental hospital. There they were apparently used to such escapades as about a dozen oddballs end up there every year. Either they act under the influence of alcohol, or they are depressives. Again, nobody took much notice of Wulf and he faded into the background until June 1985, when he made a further crossing, this time once again from West to East. The method was simple as, in spite of his previous activities, the DDR had still not bothered to improve the defences. He went to the observation platform from which he had received the cigarettes in his youth, armed with a surfboard. This he placed between platform and the top of the Wall, and simply walked across, much to the surprise of a certain Frau Fischer into whose garden he jumped. At last he was given the hearing he needed. For eight hours he had a long discussion with a member of the State Security Service which was apparently quite amiable – the inquisitor took on the role of father confessor. After this he spent ten days in a mental hospital before the Red Cross bus came to pick him up, as a valued customer. Today he gives lectures in West Berlin and probably still ponders about the challenge of the Wall – in his dreams and in his poetry.

Bibliography

Anon., *Berlin im Überblick* (Informationszentrum, Berlin, 1984)

Anon., *Ich war Grenzaufklärer* (Verlag Haus am Checkpoint Charlie, n.d.)

Anon., *13 August 1961* (Bundesandstalt für gesamtdeutsche Aufgaben, n.d.)

Anon., *Berlin – Friedrichstrasse 20.35 Uhr* (Hohwacht Verlag. Bad Godesburg, 1965)

Bath, Matthias, *Gefangen und freigetauscht* (Olzog Verlag, Munich, 1981)

Cate, Curtis, *The Ides of August* (Weidenfeld and Nicolson, London, 1978)

Clay, Lucius D., *Decision in Germany* (Heinemann, London, 1950)

Kardoff, Ursula von, *Richtig reisen – Berlin* (Dumont Verlag, Cologne, 1982)

Finn, Gerhard and Julius, Liselotte (eds), *Von Deutschland nach Deutschland* (Bundeszentrale für politische Bildung, Bonn, 1983)

Hildebrandt, Rainer, *Berlin – von der Frontstadt zur Brücke Europas* (Verlag Haus am Checkpoint Charlie, Berlin, 1984)

Hildebrandt, Rainer, *Es geschah an der Mauer* (Verlag Haus am Checkpoint Charlie, Berlin, 1984)

Hildebrandt, Rainer, *Die Mauer spricht* (Verlag Haus am Checkpoint Charlie, Berlin, 1985)

Petschull, Jürgen, *Die Mauer* (Grüner und Jahr, Hamburg, 1981)

Rühle, Jürgen and Holzweissig, Gunter (eds), *13 August 1961* (Edition Deutschland Archiv, Cologne, 1981)

Shadrake, Alan, *The Yellow Pimpernels* (Robert Hale, London, 1974)

In addition, use has been made of press-cutting files held by the Ministry for Inner German Affairs, Bonn, back numbers of magazines such as *Der Spiegel*, *Stern* and *Quick*, and original interview material obtained for the television programme, 'Hanni sends her Love'.

Index

INDEX

INDEX

210 Minuten Angst

Eine Ärztin und ihr Kind und zwei Männer berichten über ihre tollkühne Flucht, die mit einer Ehrenrunde auf dem Kudamm endete

Glücklich nach der Flucht: Winfried Kretzschmar, Hans-Jörg Fenk, Sebastian, Karl-Friedrich Fenk, Eveline Fenk. Foto: Decker (v. l. n. r.)

Berlin, 11. Dez.
Im Anhänger-Versteck eines 38-Tonnen-Lastwagens sind drei Erwachsene und ein dreijähriges Kind aus Thüringen über den Grenzübergang Drewitz ("DDR") nach Berlin geflohen. Nach der Flucht drehten sie als erstes eine Ehrenrunde über den Kudamm.

"Die dreieinhalb Stunden Fahrt waren bei erbärmlicher Kälte eine einzige Angsttour", erzählt die 26jährige Kinderärztin Eveline Fenk. Sie ist im 5. Grad schwanger.

Eveline flüchtete mit ihrem Ehemann, Hans-Jürgen, 31, ihrem Sohn Sebastian, 3, und Winfried Kretzschmar. Eine Plastiktüte voller Dokumente und eine kleine Tasche Babywäsche – das war alles, was sie als Freiheit mitbrachten.

Die Ärztin: "Wir verständigten uns in dem präparierten Anhänger nur mit Handzeichen. Wir wußten, wenn man uns erwischt, kommen wir sofort ins Gefängnis – und Sebastian in Zwangserziehung."

Karl-Friedrich Fenk, 30, der Bruder von Hans-Jürgen, lebt im Westen. Er hatte die Flucht vorbereitet und die Familie geholt.
Im September letzten Jahres fing er als Fernfahrer bei einer Westberliner Firma an.

Karl-Heinz Fenk, der 1976 ausreisen durfte: "Ich bin jeden Tag die Transitstrecke gefahren, habe überlegt, wie es klappen könnte. Dann war es soweit. Der Treffpunkt wurde vereinbart."

Die Fluchtpläne zwischen beiden Brüdern wurden in der Tschechoslowakei geschmiedet.
Eveline Fenk: "Am Kontrollpunkt bekam mein Sohn Sebastian plötzlich einen Schreikrampf. Ich hielt ihn fest, die Männer warfen Decken über mich. Als der Laster vom "DDR"-Zoll überprüft wurde, hörte Sebastian vor Erschöpfung auf zu schreien."

Inzwischen sind die Flüchtlinge per Flugzeug nach Hannover gereist.

Hier erhielten sie bereits von der Polizei ihre Ausweise.

Angler ziehe Flüchtling n Koffer aus eisigen Hav

Ch. L. Berlin, 10. Jan.
Die waghalsige Flucht nach West-Berlin gelang gestern einem 17jährigen. Der junge Mann, Jürgen K., überkletterte gegenüber der Bootsanlegestelle Moorlake die "DDR"-Mauer und schwamm durch die etwa 200 Meter breite Havel zum Westufer. Nach 20 Minuten Todesangst zogen zwei Angler und ein Kellner des Ausflugslokal "Moorlake" den völlig Erschöpften aus dem nur fünf Grad warmen Wasser. Der Flüchtling schwamm nur mit einem Arm, mit dem anderen hielt er einen Koffer fest.

Auf der Hälfte der Strecke verließen den Schwimmer die Kräfte. Er rief um Hilfe. Die "DDR"-Grenzsoldaten hatten zu diesem Zeitpunkt noch nichts von der Flucht bemerkt. Die drei Männer am Westufer riefen dem 17jährigen zu, er möge durchhalten und warfen ihm schließlich einen Rettungsring entgegen. Schließlich zogen "... mit seinem Koffer aus

auf dem Steg, w aufstehen. Später Hoppe: "Ich habe und bin in die Dauer Wirtshaus gerannt

Die beiden A der "Berliner M gen 12 Uhr sahe Mann, als er " überkletterte." 1 und Robert B kurz zuvor ihre worfen. Sie sta gestieg Moorlak kolskoer Weg.

Jürgen K. se den aus, nac Mauer mit sein Wasser gestieg Westen geschc ziergänger, wel lern alarmiert Wirtshaus 200 Meter vo fernt liegt. I pe (35) rief an. Dann ka um zu helfe

---

Sprint über den

DIETER DOSE, Berlin
Sonntag nachmittag am Berliner Ausländerübergang Checkpoint Charlie in der Friedrichstraße. Normaler Verkehr, auf der Ostseite normale Abfertigung der ein- und ausreisenden Fahrzeuge. Privatwagen, Omnibusse.

48 Stunden vorher hatte östlich der Mauer bei den "DDR"-Grenzposten helle Aufregung geherrscht. Denn zum ersten Mal seit Jahren ist einem Bewohner der "DDR" am Checkpoint Charlie die Flucht gelungen. Wie ein Sprinter jagte der 23jährige Ostberliner Fernmeldemonteur Andreas Bratke in die Freiheit. Unversehrt kam er auf der Westseite an. Ein Zollbeamter zog ihn in das Wachhaus. Auf der anderen Seite blieb ein entgeisterter Grenzsoldat zurück, der Bratke vergebens verfolgt hatte.

Der Flüchtling kannte sich am Checkpoint Charlie aus. Der Übergang wird auf der Ostseite von den "DDR"-Behörden "modernisiert" und teilweise überdacht. Seit Mona-

ten wird d Baukolonne wacht, da Fluchtversu teilt ist. Ar den Fernm beim Umb notwendig legungen d

Rund 100 schritt von zum westli rückzulegen fahrenden M nächst so Meter aber voll im Sc schwer be (Grepos). E ke aufzuhal Schußwaffe Bratke ran Grepo hinte markierung stehen und

Zahlreic point Charl